On Looking at Photographs

ON LOOKING AT PHOTOGRAPHS

■ *A Practical Guide* ■

David Hurn/*Magnum*
in conversation with Bill Jay

LENSWORK
PUBLISHING
2000

First Printing, January 2000

ISBN #1-888803-09-6

Published by LensWork Publishing, PO Box 22007, Portland, Oregon, 97269-2007

Printed in the United States of America

Acknowledgements

Our thanks to...

Molly Patrick, research assistant at Arizona State University, for her valuable help in the preparation of the manuscript.

Chris Segar, producer for Forest Films in Wales, for his exacting reading of the text and for his many astute comments.

And to the fine photographers whom we have been privileged to meet, and often call friends, whose conversations and images are continual inspirations.

David Hurn/Bill Jay

Contents

INTRODUCTION

Never, we have been told, begin writing with a negative. But rules were made to emphasize their exceptions and so we will begin by stating that this is not a how-to-do-it book in the usual sense.

It is not a textbook on how your camera works, on which lens to buy, how to mix up a developer or make an exhibition enlargement. In fact, it is not technical at all. There are plenty of good books like that already on the market.

But it *is* a how-to-do-it book in an unusual sense.

Its purpose is to suggest how to look at photographs, how to understand them, how to think about them, and, as a result, how to use photography more effectively in your daily life. It is a step-by-step appreciation course on photography, its basic principles and the characteristics which make it a unique visual medium.

In brief, *On Looking at Photographs* aims to answer the question: What is photography? and demonstrate that photography is a rich, vibrant, complex tool in the hands of intelligent practitioners.

It would be a mistake, however, to assume that this book is directed towards photographers alone. Photographs are so ubiquitous in this day and age that we, whether or not we even own a camera, are all picture-consumers. Photography is a constant and natural part of our visual environment, and we cannot escape it. Its images shape our political views, entertain us in moments of relaxation, inform our minds, illustrate our reading, help us choose between items in the market place, create images of fantasy which mould our identities, give instruction on a bewildering variety of topics from growing roses to building a boat, encourage contemplation in art galleries and museums, transport us to previously unknown destinations — and sometimes encourage us to visit the place for ourselves — take us on voyages of discovery beneath the sea, inside the human body and into outer space, provide security in our banks and other high-risk locations, and perhaps most importantly of all, allow us to capture, and hold permanently, the image of someone or something which we value highly.

We are all, everyday, on the receiving end of the photographic process, passively soaking up those pictures which we encounter with rarely a thought on their purpose or meaning. Many of the purveyors of pictures, however, do not have our best interests at heart. In this, as in many other cases, an informed mind is the best defense. An understanding of how photographs work will make us a more intelligent, and discriminating, audience. It will also awaken and deepen our appreciation for the best photographs which we encounter. Lastly, as camera-users, it will strengthen our satisfaction in our struggles to emulate the great photographers of the past.

Succinctly, then, this book is for everyone who has ever seen a photograph…

It is not about the actual making of photographs. That topic was covered in our companion volume, *On Being a Photographer*. As in that book, this sequel is formatted as if it were a discussion between the two of us. We have been friends for over thirty years and we have discussed these issues so many times that it is difficult to know who said what, when — or who generated which idea. It does not matter. What is important is that our conversations with each other and with friends and colleagues, who are also fine photographers, have convinced us that these principles of photographic appreciation deserve a wider audience. We hope you agree.

David Hurn
Bill Jay

Chapter 1

Four Fundamental Principles Of Photography

The contemplation of things as they are
Without error or confusion
Without substitution or imposture is in itself a nobler thing
Than a whole harvest of invention.

Francis Bacon, philosopher
[Dorothea Lange tacked this quotation to her darkroom door, where it remained for over 40 years]

Bill Jay: *We should start at the beginning …*

Photography was born in 1839. Since that date photographers have scrutinized a bewildering variety of faces and places and created a mountain of images the sheer volume of which defies understanding. Not that critics and historians have not made heroic attempts to analyze, categorize and describe this plethora of photographs. Images have been segregated into movements, styles, camps and groupings; their contents have been subjected to every ***-ism*** *in the fields of literature, sociology, psychology, anthropology and every other discipline yet given a name; they have been used, and abused, by everyone with an ideological axe to grind — like verses of the Bible, it is always possible to find a photograph which proves the point.*

Specialists from practically every academic discipline are scrambling over and burrowing through those millions of photographs, hurling abuse at each other's theories, while creating rampant confusion for the rest of us.

David Hurn: But the simple fact remains that for 150 years or so the basic principles of photography have been understood and applied, at least by the better photographers, regardless of the theories of the specialists who would confuse the issue. So let us itemize them so that there is no confusion. Photography's foundation is a straightforward series of steps:

1. A subject is selected because it evokes a head or heart reaction in the photographer.

2. The image is revealed with maximum clarity for the fullest expression of the subject matter.

3. The viewfinder frame is carefully inspected in order to produce the most satisfying arrangement of shapes, from the correct angle and distance.

4. The exposure is made, and the image frozen in time, at exactly the right moment.

The result is a good photograph.

Let's put aside, for the moment, a definition of "good photograph" — we will return to that topic a little later on — and look more closely at each of these steps.

They might sound prosaic and obvious but unless they are fully understood there can be no clear appraisal of the camera's images. These steps represent the structure which holds the medium together.

The first and most important point is photography's special relationship to the subject matter. In order to understand this relationship I think we have to travel back in time to the medium's pre-history.

There is no proof that photography existed in previous histories only to be re-invented in Europe during the 1830s. But there is an abundance of myth, legend and tradition in old documents which powerfully suggest that a direct transcription of reality, unsullied by the artist's hand, had been a yearning dream for thousands of years.

During all that time, there was not a culture at any period — at least that I can find — which produced representational two-dimensional art. Art, until relatively recent times, was symbolic, ritualistic, even magical.

I agree. The quest for an exact representation of nature began among Renaissance painters. Their goal was systematically to reconstruct in two dimensions familiar objects and views with meticulous exactitude. To quote Erwin Panofsky, the renowned art historian: "The Renaissance established and unanimously accepted what seems to be the most trivial and actually is the most problematic dogma of aesthetic theory: the dogma that a work of art is the direct and faithful representation of a natural object." Leonardo da Vinci would have agreed. He wrote: "The most excellent painting is that which imitates nature best and produces pictures which conform most closely to the object portrayed."

Eventually, this goal was realized. Suddenly, in the 1830s, a dozen men on various continents, independently and simultaneously, discovered what we now call photography.

It is no coincidence that the secret was discovered at the beginning of the Victorian age. The Victorians were fanatical in their passion for facts; their satisfaction was a sharp, clear, close-up of the physical world, seen not in its entirety but as isolated details. No wonder that the microscope, telescope and camera were the three indispensable tools of the age.

Photography transcribed reality. That was enough, and the Victorians were truly appreciative. You obtain a glimpse of the awe generated by the invention of photography in the words of Jules Janin, editor of the influential magazine L'Artiste: "Note well that Art has no contest whatever with this new rival photography ... it is the most delicate, the finest, the most complete reproduction to which the work of man and the work of God can aspire."

Photography was, and still is, the ideal tool for revealing what things *look like.* The thing exists — therefore it is worth recording. Does this mean that all things have equal value? Is a photograph of a cup as significant as a photograph of the Grand Canyon? From the camera's perspective, the answer is yes. The camera sees no difference in significance between the silly and the sublime; both are recorded with the same degree of value. We can sense the bemusement, even resentment, when one of the inventors of photography remarked: "The instrument chronicles whatever it sees, and certainly would delineate a chimney-pot or a chimney-sweeper with the same impartiality as it would the Apollo of Belvedere."

At this point the photographer (as a thinking, feeling human being) enters the picture, literally. The photographer makes a conscious *choice* from the myriad of possible subjects in the world and states: "I find *this* interesting, significant, beautiful or of value." The photographer can be considered as a selector of subjects; he/she walks through life pointing at people and objects; the aimed camera shouts: "Look at that!" The photographer produces prints in order that his or her interest in a subject can be communicated to others. Each time a viewer looks at a print, the photographer is saying: "I found this subject to be more interesting or significant than thousands of other objects I could have captured; I want you to appreciate it too."

Photographers have chosen to be our eyes; they are significant subject-selectors on our behalf. But can we, should we, trust them to be our eyes on the world? On the whole, no; we have a right to say: "You might have found that subject interesting, or important, but I do not." Occasionally, the answer is yes, particularly if the photographer has pursued the same subject with love and knowledge for a long period of time: more on this point a little later.

Right now, the most important consideration is that photography cannot escape the actual. As John Szarkowski , influential past-Director of Photography at the Museum of Modern Art, has written, the photographer must "not only … accept this fact, but treasure it; unless he did, photography would defeat him." The photographer places emphasis on The Thing Itself, away from self. This is not to denigrate the role of the photographer. He/she understands that the world is full of art of such bewildering variety, incomparable inventiveness, unimaginable complexity, that it will demand all the resources of his/her heart and mind in order to recognize, react to, and record its individual parts and relationships.

But there is no denying the most banal and bewilderingly beautiful truth about photography: at its core is the subject matter. Photography's characteristic is to show what something looked like, under a particular set of circumstances at a precise moment in time.

Closely allied to the earlier quest for a faithful transcription of reality, which fired the enthusiasms of the Victorians, was the demand for detail in a photograph, which translates into image sharpness.

That's true. Photography owes its origin to this desire for detail, for information, for a close-up, impartial, non-judgmental examination of the thing itself. Early photographers recommended the examination of photographs with a magnifying glass which "often discloses a multitude of minute details, which were previously unobserved and unsuspected." Viewers marveled that "every object, however minute, is a perfect transcript of the thing itself."

An abundance of detail — image sharpness — has been a crucial characteristic of photography since its introduction. There is no denying that some critics and historians would argue that there are some, if relatively rare, soft-focus and even out-of-focus images in the history of photography but in this context we are interested in the basic bed-rock principles of the medium. In spite of the exceptions it can be asserted that from the earliest days of photography, fine detail has been an essential demand of its images, from the Victorians who counted bricks in a daguerreotype to modern satellite cameras which can read car license plates from their orbiting space stations.

We have to be careful about this point. What you are saying is true but it might imply that all photographers should use an 8x10 inch view camera because of its unsurpassed ability to record fine detail. But other photographers will, of necessity, sacrifice *optimum* sharpness for, say, the maneuverability and quickness of operation afforded by the smaller negative of a 35mm camera. Nevertheless, even a small format produces more detail that is specific to the subject than any other visual art.

That is worth emphasizing. No other medium but photography, even its aspects which employ small quick cameras, is so rooted in the recording of fine detail. It is one of the principle characteristics of the camera image. A photographer who ignores this principle either risks credibility or understands the special, and unusual, circumstances in which other considerations might preclude image sharpness.

A fundamental characteristic of a photograph, then, is its compelling clarity. This is much more important than the idea of a photograph being a simple, if accurate, document. The clarity of a perfectly focused, pin-sharp image of any subject implies that the subject had never before been properly seen. Even the most prosaic and trivial of subjects is capable of being charged with significance and meaning when seen for the first time, and a detailed photograph provokes this newness-shock no matter what the subject matter. As Emile Zola remarked: "You cannot truly say that you have *seen* something until you have a photograph of it." The subject might be trivial, in any other setting, but when photographed in such a shocking, intimate manner it implies that perhaps it is *not* trivial at all, but charged with undiscovered significance.

It must be admitted that this is both the power and the bane of photography. Since the earliest days of the medium, the prosaic and the puny have been viewed and respected as much as the exotic and magnificent. Indiscriminate recording has buried us under a gargantuan avalanche of photographs of objects and dulled the newness-shock for us all. Today the habit of collecting facts is often more significant than the facts themselves. A vivid illustration of the throw-away culture is the party-goer's pleasure in posing for Polaroids which no one wants and which are discarded with the beer cans. The ubiquitous nature of photography in our society has devalued the currency of the camera; a plethora of pictures has weakened even the most powerful to exert their magic.

An aim of this book is to regenerate the newness-shock by teaching jaded viewers how to look into, rather than glance at, a photograph. And one of the most important lessons (and do not be distracted by its self-evidence) is the photograph's ability to render *detail.*

In terms of a good photograph it is obviously not satisfactory merely to include the subject somewhere in the viewfinder and ascertain that its image is reasonably sharp. The subject may be lost against an equally sharp, cluttered background; it may be too small in the picture area to reveal required information or too large so that it becomes unintelligible through loss of context. Scores of other problems may plague the image with the result that the photograph disappoints its maker and bores the audience.

Of course, the power of the subject matter may so transcend the image's faults that the photograph is still valuable, as in the case, for example, of a newspaper reproduction of an assassination attempt. In this case, *any* image, no matter how awkwardly constructed and technically inept, is better than no image at all. But that is a special circumstance. Even in this exception, however, it could be argued that the image would be even more valuable if carefully structured.

In practically all other cases, the subject and its surroundings must be organized within the edges of the picture area so that:

1. *the subject or main point of the image is revealed with maximum clarity and*

2. *the photograph is transformed from a prosaic record into an aesthetically satisfying* picture.

And the point of good design, pleasant composition or neat arrangement is not merely to emphasize the artistic abilities of the photographer but to project the subject matter and to hold the viewer's attention for a longer time while the meaning of the image has a chance to percolate from print to mind.

It has been said, with a great deal of truth, that the difference between a snapshot and a good photograph is that in the former case the photographer was looking at the subject, unaware of the viewfinder, while in the latter case the photographer was concentrating of the edges of the frame and their relationship to the subject.

Some idea of the complexity of this principle can be gauged by a simple exercise. Stand on the opposite side of the street to a large shop window. Imagine the edges of the window are the viewfinder's frame. Watch a pedestrian walk along the sidewalk in front of the window and make a mental *click!* when the figure is in a satisfying position in relationship to the frame. Relatively simple. Now watch as groups of pedestrians pass in front of the window from opposite directions. Awareness of the exact positions of the pedestrians and their relationship to the frame is infinitely more challenging.

Imagine how much more complex the problem becomes on a crowded beach. Now, your subjects are not only passing laterally in front of a window, but also moving at every directional angle towards and away from the viewpoint. In addition, the frame is no longer static but infinitely variable through 360 degrees. To pile complexity on top of complexity, the frame is also infinitely variable in size by the spectator moving closer or further away from the subjects. Add all those factors together and good picture design, especially of uncooperating, moving people in the random flux of life, is seen to be one of the most difficult challenges of photography.

But the principle is the same even when photographing a simple close-up of a static plant. The photographer makes decisions of viewpoint, distance, camera angle and scale in order to isolate the subject and produce a satisfying arrangement of shapes within the limits of the picture area. This principle will be referred to again; suffice to say, at this stage, that good design is inseparable from good photography.

Take the case of a mother watching her child play on the beach. She suddenly notices the child's expression or gesture or attitude which prompts a sudden urge to record that moment. She extracts the camera from the picnic bag, looks at the child through the viewfinder and ... *click!* ... the picture is taken. This mother has obeyed most of the principles of good photography. She has responded to a heartfelt wish to record a subject with which she is lovingly, intimately familiar. It is a fair bet that the photograph is reasonably sharp and technically competent thanks to the marvels of modern camera design. Yet...the print remains a typically amateur snapshot, of interest only to family members. The extra step which could transform the album snapshot into a picture of wider appeal has not been taken: awareness of the viewfinder and all other areas of the image *in addition to* the main object.

It is true that many wonderful images can be found in amateur albums, but these are generally the results of accidents or chance, subsequently selected out of context by a photographer aware of picture arrangement. A good photographer is always aware of the picture design whether using a camera or viewing photographs.

The basic principle here is that photography introduced a radically new picture-making technique into the history of images. Photography relies on *selection*, not synthesis. A central act of photography, then, is the decision-making process of what to include, what to eliminate, and this process forces a concentration on the lines which separate IN from OUT (the viewfinder frame).

A slightly more sophisticated idea is that the viewfinder not only isolates the subject from its environment, but also creates spaces/shapes between the subject and the frame. These too are important to the photographer. A simple example: the subject, a pedestrian, is walking down a crowded street. Including other people in the frame might not center attention on the subject. Yet a tight picture, perfectly isolating the figure against a blank wall would not convey context or environment. It might be justifiable to allow the frame to include a part of a building, or truncated limbs, or suggestions of street furniture. These intrusions into the picture space would not belong to the subject but would (if the picture was good) contribute to the design, mood, rightness, of the image.

The viewfinder frame in photography is a precise cropping tool, segmenting life into balanced images, as well as isolating details. It creates relationships of form. But more importantly it marks photography as a *picture*-making process.

If it is important to know *what* to photograph, *how* to record it for maximum clarity, *where* to position it in the picture area, it is equally important to know *when* to release the shutter. Time is critical in most photographs. And timing can be crucial whether talking of the season of the year, the time of day, or the precise fraction of a second.

Historians have noted the inordinate number of early landscape photographs which feature leafless, bare branches of winter trees. Were these photographers expressing romantic notions of man's stark destiny? Not a bit of it. They photographed many trees in winter because their exposure times were commonly 20 seconds and such long exposures tended to produce unacceptable blurs when the foliage was blowing in the breeze. In this case sharp detail was more important than prettiness for its own sake. So they waited for the leaves to fall.

Sometimes photographers could not wait for immobility. In the early days of photography with long exposure times, this led to some curious results — images which had never been seen before. A horse shook its mane and appears headless while standing the shafts of a cart; a baby squirmed and spread its features into a hazy blur as if the mother was exuding spirit-plasma; a pedestrian walked in front of the camera and became transparent as if dematerializing; and so on. These are now viewed as historical curiosities; they were then the failures.

By the 1880s, exposure times could be reduced to fractions of a second — and photographers learned that there was no such thing as an instantaneous image. All photographs are time exposures, of shorter or longer duration, relative to the speed of the subject. But they also discovered another important characteristic of photography: snapshots could freeze a moving subject in an attitude which could not be seen by the unaided eye. In fact, this ability of the camera was extremely disturbing to some viewers. When photographs were first seen which depicted people walking in a street, the viewers were aghast at the awkward, ungainly, ugly motions of bodies and limbs. How vulgar!

Photographers have always delighted in exploiting this type of newness-shock, freezing thin slices of time which could not be seen by the eye alone.

In recent decades two photographers in particular have brought wonder into photography through their use of timing. Harold Edgerton, inventor of the strobe, has revealed to us miraculous moments of rapidly moving objects, such as bullets passing through apples, balloons and light bulbs; a baseball bat bending at the moment of impact with the ball; the beautiful coronets of a splash of milk; hummingbirds in flight with even wingtips frozen; a football grossly distorted by the kicker's boot. Of course, his exposure times are not found on the average camera's shutter — his images are commonly achieved in fractions of a micro-second.

Perhaps more useful to photographers without access to sophisticated electronic strobes, is the magic of Henri Cartier-Bresson. More than any other single photographer he learned, and taught succeeding generations of photographers, how to discover the momentary patterning of lines and shapes previously concealed within the flux of life. He called this visual climax of rightness in a picture, the decisive moment. Surrounded by motion, from a score of sources, Cartier-Bresson learned how to precisely, deftly, extract a beautiful, perfect, interrelationship of expressions, gestures and shapes all interlocking into a masterful design within the picture frame.

This is the crucial difference between a mere snapshot and a fine picture of the same subject: the former reveals the subject; the latter not only reveals the subject but also catches it at precisely the instant that there is a rightness to the pattern of lines and shapes bounded by the edges of the frame.

The four fundamental principles of photography constitute the foundation posts on which the whole history of the medium is built. They were the reasons why photography was invented in the 19th century and the reasons for the astonishing growth of the camera's images into every nook and cranny of our modern world.

This would be a simple statement to verify, but a hypothetical experiment must suffice to demonstrate the point. Let us imagine the largest exhibition of photography the world has ever seen. The images are gleaned by asking the most respected professional picture-people (curators, historians, picture editors, museum directors, art directors, educators, as well as photographers) to submit their choice of "the best photographs in the history of the medium." The result would be, say, 100,000 photographs of all types from all periods.

We do not think there is *any* doubt that the vast majority of these images would be based on the principles we have described.

But would there be any images that were not at or near the medium's core characteristics? Yes, of course.

Although extremely rare, some of history's best-known images deliberately flout, for example, the principles of sharpness. I am thinking of several portraits by Julia Margaret Cameron. She infamously refused to use the standard brace-and-clamp, employed to keep the sitter's head immobile during the long exposure times necessary when working with the slow collodion process, especially on large plates. Her celebrated portrait of the scientist, John Herschel, is a good example.

It is a fine image but I am not convinced that it is any better for being blurred than sharp.

I agree. Critics have been too willing to accept without examination Cameron's notion that such technical aberrations reveal the so-called inner man. Personally, I do not see why the inner man, if it exists, is not better revealed by a sharp image.

In fact, the more I try to think of exceptions to the sharpness rule, I am increasingly aware that they hardly exist at all in any quantitative sense.

I suppose the historian would point to such images and movements as George Davison's The Onion Field *of 1890, which was made with a pinhole camera, its fuzzy image ushering in the Pictorialist movement. Many Pictorialists deliberately suppressed fine detail by various processes and surfaces in the effort to make their work more "artistic." More recently there were the out-of-focus images by Frederick Sommer and the even more recent craze for pictures taken with the Diana camera and its cheap plastic lens. But these are stylistic quirks, interesting but ultimately failed experiments or attempts at differentness for its own sake. Often these images are valued because they are rare and different.*

There will always be debate over these issues. And rightly so. The important point is that our four fundamental principles are not intended to dictate rules. They merely constitute the medium's core characteristics. They delineate the characteristics which define photography as a unique, separate, different medium. But the further the practitioner moves away from this core then the less the *photographic* principles apply until the images merge and overlap into other media and must be judged by these other criteria.

That is more difficult to explain in words than it is to recognize in practice. For example, there is no fathomable reason why a brilliant painter should not incorporate photographic imagery into his/her artistic work. The result might be wonderful. The danger comes when the work is assessed as a photograph rather than as a painting. Then two media are not competing, not antagonistic, not better-or-worse, just different.

We will have a lot more to say about art and photography in a later chapter but for now, suffice to say that a clearer idea of photography's power, and how to assess it, will emerge if the fundamental principles are kept in mind while reading the subsequent words.

Chapter 2

Meaning, And Why It Is So Slippery

We all write too much, speak too much, preach too much. It would be better if we just said what we have to say in photography. After all, we are photographers; if our work has "what it takes" it will not need the embalming of words to perpetuate it ... I believe that we do not need any justification in type for our adventures in silver. Presumably we are all afraid of something. I am probably afraid that some spectator will not understand my photography — therefore I proceed to make it really less understandable by writing defensibly about it.

Ansel Adams

Bill Jay: *Important discoveries, like photography, do not arise haphazardly, without compelling reason, or out of context. And once born their fundamental characteristics are, to a large extent, set and unchanging. We can liken this phenomenon to the genetic code of an individual which sets the foundation for appearance and aspects of attitude and behavior. In humans, of course, these characteristics can be modified by circumstances and environment. In the same way, the genetic code of photography, outlined in the previous chapter, undergoes some transformations when the images are set loose into the culture. Now we should talk about the ways in which photographs interact with viewers because they can never be seen objectively.*

David Hurn: That's true. It is like one of the fundamental principles of quantum physics: the scientist is a participant of the experiment, not an objective witness, and the result is often determined by his/

her expectations. The same is true of observers of photographs. But we should start with the simplest of premises: Photography is a form of communication.

I doubt if many viewers would disagree with this statement. It is remotely possible that someone would take the trouble to paint a frame on a spectacle lens and mentally click! when it enclosed an interesting subject — but I doubt it. The fact that photographers load their cameras with film, worry about the correct exposure, develop the negatives, and spend time and effort in making craftsman-like prints emphatically demonstrates that they wish to communicate *something* to *someone*.

There would not be much point in mastering the complex ritual and processes of photography unless the image had a purpose.

We should point out that for many photographers (perhaps the majority!) the intended audience for the pictures is one: the photographer alone. And the purpose of the photographic act is simply the pleasure in the process of doing it. That is a fair and noble purpose but does not concern us here because we, as viewers, are unlikely to see the results. As soon as viewers outside the maker are involved then the communicative role of the photograph is engaged.

Photography communicates. Agreed. But communicates what? to whom? for what purpose?

Photography — like all other media and skills — is ideally suited to some forms of communication but, it must be admitted, is totally unsuitable for others. Music, for example, is in no jeopardy from photography.

In its most fundamental sense, a photograph communicates what the subject looked like, under the particular circumstances which pertained at the moment of exposure. Throughout the medium's history the most basic and broadest function of photographs has been their substitute for the tangible presence of reality. Photographs provide a more convenient, cheaper, simpler, more permanent, and more clearly visible and useable version of the subject.

One of my favorite Victorian photographs, by George Washington Wilson, clearly illustrates this idea. It depicts a view of Queen Victoria's bedroom at Balmoral Castle, her favorite retreat after the death of her beloved Albert. On the pillow, next to her own, we can clearly see a photographic portrait of Albert alongside which she slept. It is a poignant testimony to the substitute reality power of photography. Incidentally, it is also a wonderful example of the importance of photography's reliance on detail — even though the photograph within the photograph is relatively tiny, Albert is clearly seen and recognizable.

Early painters quickly understood this ability of the camera. They directed the pose of a model and a photographer produced the picture. From then on, the painter could substitute the photograph for the model and study the pose at leisure without the cost and inconvenience of using a live sitter.

A good example is the collaboration of the painter Eugene Delacroix with the daguerreotypist Eugene Durieu. Delacroix arranged the models, Durieu photographed them and thereafter the painter had a visual reference without the presence of the models. The photograph replaced reality.

The vast majority of photographs in the history of the medium have been employed for similar purposes.

So far these examples communicate factual information which is objective not interpretive. But it is only a small step to take before facts become opinion, objective evidence becomes subjective interpretation and the context of the image distorts its message. The best way to understand this process is in these two declarative statements:

> *What a photograph is OF, is objective, factual and specific.*
>
> *What a photograph is ABOUT, is subjective, interpretive and personal.*

Now we will look at some of the many, many ways in which photographs are interpreted due to the context in which they are seen.

One of the most common problems is the (incorrect) assumption which arises from the communicative power of photography that the image can be read, like a story. It is difficult to understand how this misconception arose, yet it is certainly prevalent. Most viewers expect a photograph to be narrative, in the sense that it imparts a message, and then feel frustrated and somehow excluded from the circle of initiates, if the story cannot be deciphered.

Indicative of this assumption is the suggestion that the rise of photography heralded the death of narrative painting, as if the photograph usurped the painting's role because it was better suited for the purpose. This is odd because photography has rarely even attempted to be narrative in function. There are occasional efforts which are not renowned for their success. One daguerreotypist attempted to illustrate the Lord's Prayer in a series of photographs. The photographs are known precisely because they are such rarities. Also it is doubtful if anyone could have guessed their intent on the basis of the pictures alone. Beginning in the late 1850s a few photographers (notably Oscar Rejlander and Henry Peach Robinson) attempted narrative photographs by combining several images onto one print. The results are fascinating to historians but often completely indecipherable to present-day viewers. They remain quaint eccentricities.

Even the heroic efforts of photographers in the 1950s to combine images into sequences — picture stories — were relatively short-lived. They produced magnificent pictures but their value as story-tellers, without the accompanying captions, is very small.

Here's a simple exercise to prove the point: open an anthology of (say) war photographs at random and immediately cover up the caption/text. Now attempt to deduce the story from the image. Without prior knowledge of the event, it would be impossible.

To reiterate, photographs do not tell stories and they are not narrative in function. Photographs, instead, make verbal stories real. They evoke the sensation of reality by acting as a substitute for a direct confrontation with the subject.

Photographs are not stories but pictures.

For exactly the same reason that photographs are not ideally suited to communicating a narrative, they are not suited to communicating ideas. A great deal of pseudo-intellectual jargon has been written about photographs in an effort to prove that they impart moral messages, philosophical lessons or otherwise carry heavy intellectual weight. The usual result is to make both the text and the photographs unintelligible. Herbert Read has noted that the visual arts operate through the eyes, "expressing and conveying a sense of feeling." He continues that "if we have ideas to express, the proper medium is language." This fact, says Read, "cannot be too strongly emphasized."

This fact should also be emphasized in this context because of the prevalent assumption that photographs communicate ideas. In order to communicate ideas, or stories, photographs need words.

Before continuing with this line of inquiry, it is useful to clear up a possible source of confusion. Photographers often talk about the amount of information in a picture. This implies that the image is imparting knowledge or even verbal ideas. The implication would not be true. Photographic information is the amount of detail in a picture, the ability of the eye to separate small areas. It therefore means *visual* information. Similarly when photographers talk about facts, they mean *visual* facts i.e., how closely the image looked like reality, not facts in the encyclopedic sense.

To reiterate, photographs are not very good at communicating stories or ideas — but they are exceptionally good at communicating the up-close reality of the person or event. They provoke powerful feelings and make the subject there in our minds. This is the reason why many of the most moving and evocative photographic essays in recent decades have been bereft of explanatory text. They not only reveal strong personal emotions about people and places, but also exist as powerful pictures in their own right. Their first destination is the heart, not the brain.

The most important reason for photography's ability to create a compelling feeling about the subject is precisely because it is so inextricably linked to reality. Painters create images from imagination; writers can work from memory; musicians listen to the sounds inside their heads; only photography, distinct from all other arts and means of communication, demands the actual presence of the thing itself in front of the camera. This means that the subject, if recorded with photographic fidelity, retains a special relationship to reality. Psychologically, the viewer accepts the photograph as a valid substitute for the original subject.

Of course, we all know that photographs (and photographers) can lie. But we also know that the camera, normally operated, cannot lie. Therefore, in the presence of a photograph we all tend to suspend cynicism, accept its truth, and believe.

In a word, a photograph inspires trust. For precisely this reason photographs are constantly being presented to us as evidence or proof. A car accident reported in a local newspaper becomes real because of the image accompanying the report; the corpse was found by an office desk because the police photographs confirm the fact; the hydrogen bomb did explode as predicted because we have all seen the mushroom cloud in a photograph; a friend did visit Paris as claimed because there he/she is, standing in front of the Eiffel Tower. We can all conjure up in our mind's eye an image of a panda, an Egyptian pyramid, a steam engine, a nautilus shell, a Model-T Ford, a WW II aircraft spewing bombs, an

Indian beggar, and a myriad of other objects, even though we have never seen any of these people, animals or places in reality. Yet there is no doubt in our minds that our images are truthful and realistic — and that is because the images were lodged in our minds by previously seen *photographs* and we trusted them implicitly.

Is such faith in the veracity of a photograph misplaced? On the whole, it is not. Given the integrity of the photographer and the absence of vested interest on the part of the distributor or publisher, it is fair to say that photographs usually conform to our trust. Having seen a photograph of a white-tail deer in a nature magazine I am likely to identify it when I encounter one in the woods, and not mistake it for an elk.

Of course, there is another category of photography where vested interest makes all images suspect — advertising. But in this case we are on our guard, and know that the image has been created and manipulated to produce an idealized view of the product. Only the naive and gullible would accept such photographs at face value; the rest of us *know* that the product photograph has been manipulated to stress its strengths and hide its weaknesses.

Apart from these images, in which the creators exploit our trust in the believability of the photograph, there are several ways by which photography can lead us to incorrect assumptions inadvertently.

All photographs can be likened to quotes out of context. The photographer's basic creative act is to choose: what shall be included in, what shall be rejected, from the frame? The viewfinder defines content and therefore the photographer is constantly editing the text of the world.

By isolating two objects in the same frame, the photographer has created a relationship which might not be truthful. For example, two individuals, strangers, who happened to pass each other at a cocktail party, could be proved to be intimate friends.

Quoting out of context may merely isolate, and concentrate attention on, a salient fact, a truth about the world. It can also be dangerous. The verses of the Bible hold important insights and truths; they often are, in addition, as Samuel Johnson remarked, the last refuge of the scoundrel.

In a former career I happened to be a picture editor of a large circulation magazine. I was once asked to use a photograph of a demonstration, with faces and limbs filling every corner of the frame. It implied that hundreds of thousands of people were crowding the streets. In fact, I happened to witness the event and the total number of protesters was no more than one hundred. By isolating the few, with a telephoto lens, the photographer had given a totally different impression from the truth. Of course, the opposite impression could have been created at a mass demonstration. If the personal agenda of the editor had so willed it, the photographer could have isolated a few sparse stragglers and implied the turn out was restricted to a few malcontents.

All photographs represent a selective judgment on the part of the photographer. Whether or not the quote is apt or accurate is always difficult to judge without first-hand knowledge of the circumstances. It is as well to remember that framing is a subjective act.

The photographer Dorothea Lange once made two photographs — almost identical — of a kiva at a Southwestern pueblo. The first is a simple record of an Indian adobe building which would gracefully illustrate any article on the pueblo culture. The second photograph was taken from a few paces further back — and shows the foreground littered with tin cans. Were they dropped by uncaring, unfeeling tourists? Or by Indians, who no longer respected the old customs? We will never know, because Lange has since died. But the point remains that a slight change of viewpoint produced a large change in meaning.

There is another context in which photographs must be considered and questioned. We have seen that the subject is isolated out of its context in the natural world and that this may pose problems. In addition, all photographs are examined in the special context of the viewer's social environment, education, political persuasion, income and aspirations. If no photograph is completely objective then nor is any viewer. We all have subtly tinted filters between our eyes and minds which color all our perceptions, including our viewing of photographs. In philosophical parlance, we all suffer from intentionalism; we see what we want to see, or are led to expect.

A wonderful illustration of this point is a photograph by Robert Doisneau, At the Cafe, Chez Fraysse, Rue de Seine, Paris, 1958. *It depicts a middle-aged man standing next to a young, attractive woman at a bar. It was first published in a magazine article on Paris cafes; then in a brochure on the evils of alcohol published by a temperance league (because there are four glasses of wine in front of the couple); then in a newspaper accompanying a story on prostitution in the Champs Elysee. The meaning of the picture has changed from context to context. Its meaning will also change according to the person viewing it. In a very telling sentence, one critic wrote: "Regardless of historic fact...a picture is about what it appears to be about, and this picture is about a potential seduction." Perhaps revealing more about himself than about the image, the critic continued:*

> The girl's secret opinion of the proceedings [the potential seduction] so far is hidden in her splendid self-containment; for the moment she enjoys the security of absolute power. One arm shields her body, her hand touches the glass as tentatively as if it were the first apple. The man for the moment is defenseless and vulnerable; impaled on the hook of his own desire, he has committed all his resources, and no satisfactory line of retreat remains. Worse yet, he is older than he should be, and knows that one way or another the adventure is certain to end badly. To keep this presentiment at bay, he is drinking his wine more rapidly than he should.

This might be a fine example of creative writing but it has little to do with the actual photograph. As I understand the circumstances, Robert Doisneau arranged and set up the scene with model friends. But the image, of these particular people at this particular location, at this particular time, is about whatever the viewer believes. This is what the fancy term semiotics is all about.

We should not forget the cultural context in which photographs are seen. A simple example: Louis Bernal was a fine photographer who made a special study of the living conditions of Chicanos, or Spanish-Americans, in the rural Southwest. Many of his photographs were funded by the Federal Government (through the National Endowment for the Arts) and exhibited nationally in galleries and museums. *In this context*, the expected and received response from white, middle-class viewers was a more real awareness of the poverty and distress of a segment of the American public. The photographs elicited sympathy in the plight of Chicanos. But now let us change the viewing context and present these same photographs to those unfortunates living in the streets of Calcutta, or the shacks of Mexico City, or the refugee camps of Asia. These viewers would undoubtedly have a far different reaction to the photographs than the middle-classes of America. The homeless would envy the Chicanos their sturdy walls, with glass windows covered by floral drapes, their family momentos in private rooms, even their television sets. In the first context the photographs mean poverty; in the second context they mean unimaginable luxury.

All photographs have similar contexts for understanding. They do not exist as isolated entities. Every one of them makes reference to the photographer's biography, the subject's demands, the social environment, the age in which it is produced, and the viewer's response which is molded by viewing context.

This is such a crucial point in our effort to understand photographs that it is worth mentioning several of these factors in more specific terms.

We all see photographs through our personal prejudices. We cannot switch off our life-attitudes at will when looking at pictures and they are therefore altered in meaning by the process of viewing.

I once worked for an editor who had an antipathy for swans and therefore no swan photograph was ever allowed to be published in the magazine. (Not that there was any overwhelming need to ever include a swan in any article for any reason). I do not think any of our readers noticed their omission or would have cared had they done so. In other cases, personal prejudice is much more problematic and might even lead to a gross distortion of the truth.

I am reminded of a lecture which we attended together. It was by an art historian who, as an avowed lesbian, was anxious to find evidence of lesbianism in 19th-century photography. Needless to say, she found plenty — at least to her own satisfaction. For example, she discovered the photographs of Clementina, Countess of Hawarden, nearly all of which depict young ladies, often with their arms around each other. The evidence disputes her conclusion, based solely on visual clues. Lady Hawarden's subjects were her own daughters. Obviously, the interpretation of images by the lecturer, and not the historical facts, had dictated their meaning.

Photographs do not carry around with themselves, like excess baggage, a particular meaning. They are more circumspect and difficult to pin down than that. They are adaptable and often feel comfortable among very different neighbors, shifting allegiances depending on the aims of the group with which they happen to reside at the time.

A simple experiment which I often present to students will illustrate the point. A group of, say, twenty slides depicting rocks, water, sand, surf, reflections is selected and projected with biographical notes and quotations by Minor White. All the photographs are fine images and no student ever doubts that one of the slides is not by the artist but is an unidentified and prosaic record by the United States Air Force, taken in 1945, depicting an aerial view of mud flats. Even when the students are told that one of the Minor White pictures is a fake, the prosaic record is rarely distinguished from the fine art images. This experiment could be conducted with any number of photographers. For example, a Paul Strand lathe picture (fine art) is indistinguishable from many commercially made lathe publicity photographs (prosaic records) supplied by engineering companies.

The point of the exercise is not to denigrate the photographer's works but to emphasize that pictures which look alike may have different functions and meanings depending on the viewing context.

A colleague was challenged by students: "When is a photograph a work of art?" He replied: "When it is hanging on an art gallery wall."

There is a great deal of truth to this seemingly flippant answer. The viewing conditions channel the spectator's minds into a certain expectation from the photographs. In the case of a pristine cavernous gallery, with an atmosphere of hushed reverence, perhaps associated with the great art of past ages, when viewing flawlessly made prints in precious overmats and carefully isolated frames, we are induced to mentally approach the photographs from a particular angle: ART, with all the connotations which this word implies. We carry the expectations of viewing art to the photograph; the photograph is not thrusting it out at us. In another context, exactly the same photograph, to the same mind, would carry *no* art associations. Meaning has altered with the photograph's context.

The meaning of a photograph is not intrinsic to the image. In other words, there is no correct interpretation of a particular photograph, under all conditions, in every context, to every viewer.

Another factor affecting meaning is the mere passage of time. Many photographs taken in the 19th century, and considered by contemporaneous viewers as prosaic, uninteresting and even wasteful images, have since become fascinating pictures, of immense value to historians and delightful curiosities to modern viewers — because the subject matter no longer exists. In these instances, nostalgia is the power of the picture. To anyone interested in women's fashion almost every Victorian photograph of a crinoline is of interest. The original picture was probably made as a prosaic family portrait; the image today is viewed for the clarity of the dress design — and the individual wearing the crinoline is of marginal interest. The emphasis has dramatically shifted through the age of the image.

Most early photographs are invariably viewed through a nostalgic haze which markedly alters the value of the image away from the photographer's original intent.

A more fundamental shift in image meaning occurs through time due to visual conventions. In each age, there exists an unstated but acknowledged circle of possibilities within which the image style is acceptable and beyond which the image appears unacceptable, if not absurd. Gradually, through the passage of time, this circle also moves. Previously accepted stylistic appearances appear old-fashioned and the previously unacceptable style is absorbed and contained, becoming the norm.

We have already remarked that the first photographs of people walking in the street (around 1859) might have been admired for their technical accomplishment (in an age when exposure times were measured in several seconds) but they were also deplored for the ugly, ungainly actions of the pedestrians. Contemporary viewers were aghast that people, including themselves, appeared so awkward in their movements; the visual convention of the age had not included natural bodily actions.

A more striking example concerns images of horses in motion. Prior to the 1870s paintings of trotting and galloping horses were all depicted in exactly the same style: a hobby-horse attitude with front and rear legs stretched out. This was the visual convention, the consensus of opinion on how a horse in motion *should* be depicted. In the late 1870s a photographer, Eadweard Muybridge, proved conclusively that at *no* time during the action does a horse adopt this hobby-horse attitude. The convention was broken. A new visual truth was agreed, at least by the majority of painters. For a few, the visual convention was rigidly held and they preferred the lie.

Such examples of visual conventions of the age are clearly understood in retrospect. It is far more difficult, if not impossible, to acknowledge that we all look at photographs today in relationship to the visual conventions of our age. The seemingly insurmountable problem is to identify and isolate these visual conventions, and to assess how they are influencing the meaning of an image, while we are living in that age. Perhaps the only answer is to acknowledge the presence of such conventions and understand that the meaning of contemporary images will change with time, in ways that we cannot even begin to predict. The original caption, or accompanying text, provides us with a benchmark to original meaning, and that is why documentation is so valuable to historians.

It is worth reiterating that in order for a photograph to tell a story or impart an idea, as opposed to revealing emotion, the image must be accompanied by words. Because of the suspension of disbelief associated with a photograph the accompanying words also tend to evoke veracity by their close proximity to the image. Yet we all know the ease with which words can create misunderstandings, or be downright lies. Conversely, accurate words often transform an otherwise incomprehensible image into a powerful, evocative and memorable story or idea.

I once discovered a photograph by Paul Martin which showed a group of children and a policeman in Lambeth, a working class area of London, in 1892. It was difficult to understand why the photographer had taken the picture.

Assumptions concerning the story of the picture would be even more tentative. It is likely that the children are waiting for (not actually watching) an event, because the attention of the faces is scattered. The boys in the background seem to be trying to reach a higher vantage point which probably confirms this assumption. The policeman is, perhaps, controlling the crowd. But why does the crowd comprise only children? No assumptions can be made. Is the event a happy or tragic one? No assumptions can be made — some children appear unhappy, others are smiling.

In the face of such paucity of information any reasonable caption which fits the assumptions will be accepted as true. This picture might depict the children waiting to catch a glimpse of Queen Victoria as she passes through a working-class area of London; or, these children might be inmates of a poorhouse for street urchins who are waiting for new arrivals rounded up by the police; or, they might be watching a fire, or a group of street acrobats, or a dancing bear, or any ceremony, pageant, ritual, new event, public performance or procession. The photograph does not tell us the story. Then I discovered Martin's own account of the incident. The children are indeed waiting for an event, the nature of which could never have been deduced from the image, yet the event was the raison d'etre for the photographer taking the picture at all. The children are waiting for the funeral procession of a feared policeman who terrorized the kids and whose death caused considerable public interest in the neighborhood: in the excitement of arresting a thief, the policeman swallowed his own false teeth and choked to death!

The story (in words) brings the photograph to life; the photograph (a picture) gives drama and impact to the story.

All photographs probably benefit from the addition of words, even a meager identification of place and date. When the photograph is used in a story-telling context or to illustrate an idea, words are essential.

This is such an important point to make, and one which causes a great deal of confusion even among photographers, that it is tempting to prolong the discussion by offering example after example. Limitations of space have removed the temptation. However, one more point needs to be made concerning the value of words accompanying photographs in order to tell a story.

Photographers will use as contradictory evidence the picture story idea, employed by magazines in the 1940s and 50s, which attempted to achieve narrative through a planned sequence, size relationship, and layout design of a number of photographs, and the more the better. Perhaps the most significant photographer of the picture-story was W. Eugene Smith whose essays in *Life* magazine included: *Country Doctor, Nurse Midwife, Man of Mercy,* and *Spanish Village* as well as others.

Smith's avowed intent was to force photography into the role of literature, particularly the epic poem. For his Pittsburgh story he made over 11,000 negatives in one year (1955), printed 7,000 proofs, whittled them down to 2,000 images. Eventually, the only publication willing to give him the space which he felt the project deserved and to allow him to write his own text was *Popular Photography Annual,* in 1958. It used 88 images over 34 pages. Significantly, Smith hoped to recoup the story's power through the accompanying text, which was labored, extremely tortured prose. On Smith's own terms, the whole project was a failure *as an essay*. The fact remains that W. Eugene Smith was a highly accomplished picture maker, not a story-teller. He made beautiful and compelling photographs but the accompanying words told the story while through his images the story leapt to life.

An aspect of reading photographs which is rarely mentioned, deserves a brief explanation. It is this: even the most careful and attentive viewer of photographs has a tendency to see evidence which does not exist, and neglect to see what is revealed in the photographic image. Our eyes are fickle and our brains leap to conclusions based on too little data. Photographs, by their specificity, lull us into assuming that a glance will do; the mind, reacting to a general impression, fills in the gaps and presents us with a conclusion — often erroneous.

I have an example ... There is a photograph by André Kertész that was taken in Budapest, May 19, 1920. The caption is specific, but does not tell us the picture's circumstances. At a glance I might assume that a man and a woman are looking through a hole in the wall probably at a carnival or circus. Most viewers would probably agree. Yet not a single one of these assumptions is confirmed in the photograph. Why not two women? Is there a hole in the wall? It is not evident. Why do we assume that they are looking at something on the other side of the fence? There is nothing in the photograph to confirm this observation. The point is that we all tend to read into photographs evidence that is not there. Similarly, we do not see what *is* there. Most viewers in this case do not notice that the man is one-legged — or is he?

Such mental addition and subtractions are part of picture viewing.

We could continue indefinitely in this direction, listing and illustrating many, many other factors which affect and alter the meaning of a photograph. So let us summarize.

What a photograph is OF is the visual appearance of the subject at the time of the exposure.

What a photograph is ABOUT is infinitely variable, depending on: the viewer's social environment, education, political persuasion, income and aspirations; on the photographer's and the viewer's culture, and the differences between them; on the images which precede and follow the particular image looked at; on the context in which the image is viewed, whether personal album, newspaper, art periodical, gallery, classroom, lecture hall, and so on; on the viewer's knowledge of authorship, the reputation of the image's maker, any knowledge of a critic's, historian's or teacher's comments; on the nostalgia and sense of strangeness of an image made in a previous age or alien culture; on personal, private past experiences, emotional scars, taboos — even those of which the viewer is unaware on a conscious level; on the visual conventions of the age, both when taken and when viewed; on aesthetic choices and theories.

And there are more, all of which interact, producing highly complex patterns of influence.

The conclusion which we can reach therefore is this comforting thought for the reader. If you have ever felt intimidated because there must be a single meaning of a photograph but felt you were too inexperienced to understand it, then relax. A photograph will never have a single interpretation due to the above influences. For the same reasons, no authority can insist on or convince you that a single ideological/political interpretation is the only correct one.

Think of it this way. You cannot peel away the layers of an onion until you discover its essence. The onion is its layers. Similarly, there is no essence-of-meaning in a photograph.

Chapter 3

Merit, And Why It Is So Rare

It is quite unimportant whether photography produces "art" or not. Its own basic laws, not the opinions of art critics, will provide the only valid measure of its future worth. It is sufficiently unprecedented that such a "mechanical" thing as photography, and one regarded so contemptuously in an artistic and creative sense, should have acquired the power it has, and become one of the primary objective visual forms ...

Laszlo Moholy-Nagy

Bill Jay: *In the previous section we discussed the many meanings of a single photograph and some of the factors which contribute to its elusiveness. Meaning is malleable which is why it can be deliberately manipulated in order to provoke in you, the viewer, the correct response.*

Up to now we have presumed that the photographs being discussed are on public display, whether reproduced in periodicals or shown in exhibitions. But when we begin discussing the merit of a photograph — why one picture is better than another — we need to be clear about the purpose of the picture, and take into account the fact that a successful picture is not dependent on the size of the appreciative audience.

That sounds rather nebulous. To make the point, David, we should give some specific examples.

David Hurn: I would start with an image which might have a miniscule audience but a major significance. If a doctor makes an x-ray photograph of my chest and it reveals a potentially fatal flaw which is quickly removed, I will cherish that image because it saved my life. To me, that prosaic document will have become the most important image in the history of the medium! Because it performed its required function (the accurate diagnosis of the illness) it was a good photograph. However its value is short-lived (the few minutes it took to examine the image for the flaw) and its audience was a mere two interested viewers (the doctor and myself). For the majority of x-ray photographs the image will remain of such limited appeal; for a few, however, there will be a wider audience. This x-ray may depict a rare disease and find its way into a slide lecture, medical journal or textbook for the edification of other doctors. Now and again, what started as a prosaic x-ray might be taken out of context by a visual artist and used in a conceptual art book, such as *Evidence* by Mike Mandel.

Of wider, but not general, appeal than medical records are photographs made for a community of professionals. A local newspaper recently published an astronomical photograph which looked, to my inexpert eye, to be a fuzzy white splotch in a black background, no different to many space pictures already seen. However, this particular fuzzy splotch had created immense interest among astronomers because it depicted the first alien solar system ever photographed. Without this caption the image would have been meaningless to the majority of us because we do not belong to the specialized viewers who could appreciate its significance. The audience of specialists, however, would be larger than the interested viewers for the previous picture.

In order to explore the action-stopping potentials inherent in electronic flashes of extremely short duration, the scientist Harold Edgerton displayed considerable imagination in setting up his test subjects. When he photographed a bullet in flight passing through an apple he demonstrated the frozen action ability of his specialized flash unit — but he did something more. He expanded the potential audience of a technical exercise by an imaginative use of subject matter.

Of even wider appeal are the photographs which connect all viewers by reason of their humanity. A disjointed, slightly fuzzy news photograph of a naked young girl in Vietnam, fleeing from her napalmed village became a universal symbol for the horror of war. The photograph had an interested, and concerned, audience numbering in the millions.

Note that in these examples of the expanding audience for photographs, not one has been dependent on the *aesthetic* rightness of the image. Many photographs are useful, provocative, appealing and highly symbolic — and successful in terms of their audience appeal — without reference to their rightness as aesthetic objects. In fact, many of them are "bad" pictures in any traditional sense of composition, lighting or craftsmanship. Photographs are unique in that this lack of perfection may actually contribute to the power of the images by implying their closer relationship to real life, shorn of artistic pretensions.

The opposite is also true. A photograph may have aesthetic merit alone, shorn of any pretension that the subject matter is important. For example, photographs which were taken for a limited audience, such as in a family album, can be transformed from a snapshot to a picture with general appeal because of the beauty of its interlocking forms and shapes. Consider The Beach at Villerville, *1904, taken by Jacques Henri-Lartigue. He was 10 years old. His snapshot was captured at precisely the right moment when the arrangement of figures, background, gestures, and spaces between objects was in such perfect relationships that a prosaic family holiday picture was elevated to a picture of universal appeal.*

The ideal, of course, is to combine a subject of wide appeal with a high degree of craftsmanship and visual design. This seems self-evident but it is more contentious than it appears. Photographers do indeed debate and worry about the issue of design. Some would advocate a deliberate *lack* of structure in the picture as a means of forcing a viewer's attentions on the subject matter and not on the craftsmanship or artistry of the photographer. Many times we have heard photographers explaining that one of their photographs is too beautiful as a picture and that viewers tend to concentrate on the skill with which the photograph was made while ignoring the actual subject of the image.

This is a difficult dilemma for photographers, who are obviously reluctant to deliberately make bad photographs. Nor do they. They strive for aesthetic and technical perfection, consistent with the subject matter, and hope the beauty of the image will not detract form the subject but, conversely, hold the viewer's attention longer while even more information and emotion are transmitted.

In light of these remarks I vividly remember an occasion in London in the late 1960s when we were with a group of highly respected photographers, looking at a set of prints by Don McCullin, who had just returned from war-torn Biafra. One of the images was stunning: it depicted a starving young mother (although she looked ancient) whose depleted breasts did not contain enough milk to feed her new baby. Appreciation for the picture circulated around the group: "Great picture, Don"; "Terrific image"; "A classic Madonna and child"; and similar phrases of praise. Don listened morosely and then angrily shouted: "That's not a great picture, *that's an actual young mother who is starving to death in Biafra right now!"*

This anecdote illustrates the horns of the photographic dilemma: the medium's specificity, its roots in an actual person, place and time, and its ability to simultaneously transcend the actual and become an icon for a more general, universal feeling. In our anecdote, both Don and his colleagues were correct. Don was right: the emphasis should be on the plight of the specific individual in Biafra at this specific moment in time. But his colleagues were also right: the image is so beautiful, even of a horrifying subject matter, that it transcends the literal and symbolizes suffering everywhere at any time. Ultimately it is not necessary to know the specific circumstances under which the picture was taken. It can be shorn of words, taken out of context, and symbolize the dignity and determination which guards the human spirit even in its darkest moments. It is simultaneously both tragic and uplifting.

The lesson here is that the best photographs can function in different contexts. Another, less emotional, example would be the photograph *White House Ruins, Canyon de Chelly, 1873,* by Timothy O'Sullivan. It shows an ancient Indian rock dwelling nestled in a tiny crevice, above which is the looming face of the canyon wall. It was originally taken on a geographical and geological expedition and it had a very specific purpose: to prove that the canyon was created by glacial scouring, as evidenced by the striations in the rock face, and not by volcanic upheaval. This was a contentious and hotly-debated issue at the time.

Today, no one has any knowledge of or interest in this intent. It's a great picture of the place — and also symbolizes man's puny efforts in the face of the towering power of nature, or any other subjective reaction with which the viewer might respond to it. The point is that this image is so good that it has transcended its original purpose.

In this chapter on photographic merit we have (over)used the word "good." By now the reader must be frustrated that no clear definition seems to be emerging. That is a reasonable concern so let us interject a few words on what we mean by a good photograph, acknowledging that any discussion of aesthetics is fraught with dangers and difficulties. Books have been written by many brilliant philosophers about the subject, and no two can agree on a definition of fine art or aesthetics. We intend to take the coward's way out of this maze of madness by avoiding all philosophical concepts and aestheticisms and concentrate on basic principles which will be more useful to the practising photographer and the average viewer of photographs.

In our previous book together, *On Being a Photographer,* we experienced a similar difficulty in defining what constitutes an honest approach to picture-making. We admitted we did not know — but, we did know when we were acting *dis*honestly. It is the same problem with the word "good." It is best defined by what it is *not*. For example ...

"Good" is not the same as "important."

There have been very many important photographs in the mediums history which are not "good" in any aesthetic sense.

A clear example which springs to mind is the photograph, achieved through electron microscopy, of the DNA molecule, a revolutionary discovery in the scientist's quest to unravel the secrets of life. There is no doubt that this is one of the most important photographs ever made, but one which has little aesthetic value.

"Good" is not the same as "useful."

A basic function of photography, as we have already discovered, is that it shows us what things look like. But the successful result of this function is not necessarily aesthetically pleasing. Most product photographs fall into this category.

A prosaic picture of a camera, for example, might be a success in that it clearly depicts the instrument, the position of its controls, and other features which are informative and useful. Few viewers, however, would claim the image was aesthetically good.

"Good" is not the same as "interesting."

Although the choice of subject matter is a major factor in the appeal of a photograph, even a subject of wide popular interest may be reduced to a dull, banal picture by insensitivity or incompetence on the part of the photographer.

Few subjects are as fascinating to viewers (of both sexes) as the female nude. But no one would argue that all photographs of their subject have equal merit. A few are exceptional in their aesthetic merit; most are banal and devoid of any attempt at aesthetic value. They are more akin to product photographs, in their emphasis on specific parts, than to good pictures.

"GOOD" IS NOT THE SAME AS "LIKING."

One of the most common fallacies of photographic criticism is the assumption that there is a relationship between liking an image and its merit. Such a link is understandable but erroneous. We are all more prone to like a photograph if we are interested in the subject matter, if we are curious as to how it was done, if we make our own photographs in a similar style or with the same technique, if we have a personal acquaintance with the photographer, or if we are aware of the photographer's fame. All these factors can alter, or deviate us from, an objective appraisal of the image itself.

The statement: "It is a good photograph, but I do not like it" is not paradoxical. Nor is the opposite: "It is not a very good photograph, but I like it."

As an instructive mental exercise the reader should attempt a list of photographs which he/she would include in each category.

I will give a couple of examples. Personally I do not like the aggressive street photographs taken by Gary Winogrand or the peeling-plaster/torn-poster images by Aaron Siskind. Both, widely different types of photographs, assault my own prejudices — my own preference for a compassionate view of the human race in the former, and my own inability to see anything visually interesting in design-pictures in the latter case. Yet both photographers are fine proponents of their particular area of image-making. My dislike for this work is personal and has nothing to do with their merit.

In my case, I have a collection/touring exhibition of images, all of which I find visually stimulating. Alongside prints by great photographers — such as Henri Cartier-Bresson, Bill Brandt, Don McCullin and many others — I have included prints, reproductions and postcards of pictures by anonymous photographers. They might not be considered images of high merit by some museum curators but I like them enough to include them in my personal collection.

If it was possible to provide a definitive list of factors to answer the question: what makes a good photograph?, then all photographs would tend to look very similar. The incredibly complex variety of magnificent images, however, refutes such a possibility. For every factor on a list an astute viewer would invariably think of exceptions to the rule. This fact might be frustrating to those who want specific answers to every question. Their only consolation is that it is this very diversity of photographic images which makes it such a fascinating medium.

One philosopher has noted that there are two types of problems. The first is called a convergent question. This is the type of problem about which continuous questions produce a specific answer. For example, if the problem concerned a means of transportation, powered by the human muscles, which traveled faster than a walk, it is a fair bet that the questions would eventually result in an answer which looked very much like a bicycle.

The second type of problem is called a divergent question. In this case, further questions lead away from an answer and merely lead to more questions. For example: what is the purpose of education? Or, what is a good photograph?

Having set the latter question squarely in the group of problems which have no definitive, specific answers, it is possible to provide some general guidelines as an aid to minimizing random flounderings in this murky, choppy sea.

A useful start when looking at photographs is to ask yourself three questions about the image:

1. What was the intent of the photographer?

2. How well has this intent been realized?

3. Was the intent worth the effort in the first place?

A number of contemporary critics would dispute the validity of such questions. It is, they claim, the fallacy of intentionalism. We disagree. These questions may not provide a definitive answer (no sane critic would claim that such an answer existed) but they *are* valid as a tentative first step in understanding how photographic merit is rooted in a specific purpose. From this beginning the picture can blossom into something that transcends the original intent to become a more universal, symbolic image.

Meanwhile, in our efforts to clarify some of the most important issues relating to photographic merit, we have ignored several tangential topics that deserve more detailed discussions.

That is true. And one of the important questions refers back to our first section: Has the content of the image been intelligently structured? The emphasis in this sentence should be placed on "intelligently."

There are no absolutes in picture design and anyone expecting to find a rule-book of photographic composition is sure to be disappointed. The photographer, through experience and steeped in the great images of the past, finds a rightness in the frame which is appropriate to the subject. Such appropriateness may not be specifically evident to a viewer but merely emerges as a sense of satisfaction that the image has been clearly seen and structured with intelligence.

The word that I like to use for this sense of image rightness is: inevitability. It occurs when you mentally try to improve the picture by moving around its component parts within the frame and cannot improve on the original. Then you know that it was inevitable that the picture was constructed in that way.

Actually, this is a good exercise for photographers. Look at your own pictures, as well as the images by others, and not only attempt to shift their elements to create a visually more satisfying result but also ask: would the image have been better if photographed just a fraction of a second sooner or later, and would the image be improved if I had moved a little to the left/right/up/down/closer/further back?

By asking these critical questions (and answering them truthfully!) about each and every exposed frame, the photographer gradually develops the instinct for what makes a good picture.

The good photographer also has a finely developed instinct, which again arises from continual use of the camera and critically comparing expectation with result, about the difference between seeing and photographing.

There is a good deal of sense in the old adage that a fine photographer is one who knows what *not* to photograph. Many subjects might look impressive to the eye but do not translate into a flat image on a piece of paper. I cannot think of a photograph, for example, which comes close to matching the visual awe experienced at the Grand Canyon. Every photographer has had the experience of looking at contact sheets and wondering now why on earth did I take *that* frame? The photographer must think photographically, previsualising the end result as a picture after is has been translated and scrambled by the photographic process. What you see is not the same as what appears on the print.

The fine photographer often utilizes this disparity between seeing and photographing. In other words he/she sees a photograph, an arresting image, in commonplace subject matter which would be ignored by lesser photographers. If the viewer had been standing alongside the photographer at the moment of exposure there would have been no doubt as to the nature of the subject or situation. Yet the viewer would not have seen the photograph. A great number of interesting images in the history of photography have been based on the disparity between reality and the picture. As Gary Winogrand explained, he made photographs in order to see what things looked like when photographed.

A variation of this theme is that photographers often exploit the believability of photography and a known lie. This causes a visual jolt, the image equivalent of the punch line of a good joke, or a clever aphorism. An example would be the photograph, by Cherry Kearton, of a man carrying a cow on his shoulder with all four legs of the beast stiffly pointing to the sky. The absurdity of the situation is striking; the photograph proclaims validity yet the mind refuses to accept the veracity of the image. (The explanation in this case is that the cow is a hollow hide in which the photographer can crawl and photograph birds surreptitiously).

Presumably, this photograph was deliberately made in order to produce a sense of strangeness in the minds of the viewers. The photographer saw, at the time of the exposure, the oddness of the situation and decided to record it. But so many photographs produce this effect inadvertently that it almost rises to the level of a characteristic common to fine photographs. Certainly, in so many pictures, it is an important, even crucial, element in their success.

You are right. In these cases the effort to capture the real has slipped into the surreal. Photography is particularly and peculiarly prone to producing these slippages in which a prosaic document of something, extracted from its original context, acts as a trigger to unexpected and even disconnected emotions.

One of the most potent images in my personal memory-bank is a prosaic industrial photograph taken inside a doll factory in 1918. It shows rows of unfinished dolls inside a metal oven in front of which a worker is aiming a spray-gun at a doll held in his other hand. It is by an anonymous photographer and I presume it was made as part of a series to illustrate how dolls are made. But irrespective of this original purpose it is a most disturbing image, to me. I saw it on one occasion, over thirty years ago, and it is still haunting me.

My own example would be a photograph by André Kertész, depicting the back of a black-coated man in front of a broken park bench. Almost every one who looks at this picture feels a sense of menace, yet there is not a single element in the image that is menacing per se.

Photography is such a surreal medium because similar transitions from the actual to the imagined occur so regularly. This is a very important point but one which is difficult to explain with clarity. We must delight in the fact that there is such irony in the camera, which is presumed to be such a banal fact-recorder, throws out such strangeness with such ease and frequency. No wonder the Surrealists were so enamoured with photography; they understood this quirkiness of the medium perhaps more profoundly than its practitioners. As Andre Breton, who wrote the First Surrealist Manifesto *in 1924, said: "Surrealism is contained in reality itself."*

It is certainly a wonder to cherish — that strangeness need not be prefabricated. It arises naturally from the way the camera sees the world.

One of my all-time favorite photographers is Bill Brandt who often wrote about this topic. He talked of seeing the world "as familiar yet strange;" he marvelled at the "spell that charged the commonplace"; he reveled in the fact that "the camera is much more than a recording apparatus. It is a medium via which messages reach us from another world." It is no coincidence that Brandt personally knew many of the Surrealists.

We could spend the remainder of this text extolling the virtues of this strange link between reality and the camera's images but we should move on.

I want to raise another attribute of the fine photographer. It is the tricky topic of quantity. It seems to me that one of the important characteristics is that he/she can sustain an idea over a long period of time through many, many images. The obvious conclusion to be drawn from this statement is that the better photographers shoot a lot of pictures. And that is true.

In his own inimicable way, George Bernard Shaw once remarked that a photographer is like a cod which lays a million eggs in order that one may survive. This remark has been wrongly employed by critics to attest that any fool who shoots enough pictures will eventually take a good one. True, but only one good one. Even a dog, fitted with a programmed motor-drive camera would probably take a good photograph, in time. But that is not the point.

The story which best exemplifies the idea of the value of quantity concerns a Chinese artist who was commissioned to paint a picture of a fish for a wealthy client. Months went by and the painting was not supplied. In frustration the client accosted the artist in his home and demanded an explanation. In reply the artist took a brush and pad and in a few deft strokes produced a beautiful image of a fish.

The client was still dissatisfied: how could anything so simple be valuable? In reply, again, the artist beckoned the client to a cupboard, opened the door, and out spilled thousands of paintings of fish, the essential precursors to the final image. So it is in photography.

In photography quantity goes hand-in-hand with quality. Sustaining concentration on a subject or idea over a long period of time is the photographer's way of becoming absolutely familiar and in perfect empathy with the picture-producing situation. Only then, with confidence, can the photographer be supportive of the image, assured that the struggle with the subject through many attempts has produced a satisfying picture at the limits of his/her abilities.

It would be a mistake to think that only street photographers work in this way. All photographers must pay homage to the subject through a quantity of images. Take the case of Harry Callahan's simple, elegant study of grasses in the snow. Callahan did not merely stumble across the subject, take a single negative, and move on. His archives (at the Center for Creative Photography, Arizona) contain scores of contact proof prints of exactly the same subject with minor variations; in fact he took over 500 photographs of twigs in the snow. The final image is the end result of a long struggle and lots of hard work.

In order to be able to sustain many images over a long period of time on the same theme the photographer must *care* about the subject. A photograph is the end product of someone caring about something. The best photographs exude this care in a manner which is not definable but which is very evident.

Lewis Hine, for example, was not interested in promoting himself as an artist-photographer but he did care deeply about the plight of children who were employed in dangerous environments under conditions of slave labor. He began working for the Child Labor Committee in 1907 and his photographs, badly reproduced in such tiny images that they often seem swamped by text, were published in *The American Child*. He recognized that words would tell the story, but that his photographs could make the story dramatically real. He cared, and it showed.

But this caring for the subject is not the prerogative of such emotionally charged themes as child labor. Stephen Dalton is a British entomologist-photographer who obviously has a passion for, and deep knowledge of, insects. His technically amazing, and aesthetically beautiful, images of insects in flight ooze a love for bugs even to those who have an aversion to the little beasts themselves.

Other examples would be superfluous because *all* good photographers have a deep commitment to, and involvement with, their subjects, and through photography they are communicating their understanding and passion to others.

Please read the last sentence again because it brings up a very important aspect of the best photography. If the photographer is communicating a personal passion through his pictures then the images are also revealing a great deal about the photographer as well as the subject. His /her attitude to life is evident.

On a simple level this fact is explicable merely because a photographer's choice of subject matter can be revealing of personality as well as interests. At a deeper level, the issue becomes more profound. The more intensely the photographer struggles to place emphasis on subject matter so, paradoxically, the photographer reveals a personal attitude to life itself. This is never revealed in a single photograph. However, a body of work by a photographer begins to reflect back to the viewer the author's relationship not only to the subject but also to a unique life-attitude.

This cannot be injected into a photograph by intent. Style is not like a filter which when placed over the lens will affect the image. Too many young photographers shoot a sleeping drunk in a doorway to show they care; in actuality it usually shows the opposite. A unique style emerges in photography by ignoring it, concentrating on the subject, and allowing care, passion and knowledge to bubble to the surface through a lot of hard work over a long period of time.

That is why the best photographs are truly reflective of the photographers. The pictures become extensions of the person and it is evident that a personal style has emerged, which cannot be confused with the works of any other photographer. This is not difficult to understand; it is clearly evident in the style of writers, poets or musicians. Style in photography operates in exactly the same way, in spite of this medium being more closely identified with reality.

The first paragraph referred to a life-attitude and then we switched to a discussion of style. This was deliberate because in the same way that the subject matter reflects areas of interest so a photographer's style reflects his life attitude. For example, Don McCullin is probably the greatest photographer of war that the medium has yet known. His subject matter is depressing to put it mildly. We have already mentioned one image. Starving refugees, bombed children, mutilated civilians, dying soldiers, terror-struck families and decaying corpses seem as though they should be extremely depressing images by a masochistic voyeur. Yet ... look at a large number of McCullin's horrific images and another deeper impression emerges to counteract the first shock reaction. The photographs, *en masse*, exude a dignity, pride of spirit and commitment to human values under the extreme test of their endurance. They are inspiring, and in spite of the subject matter, elevate the spirits and reaffirm or even elevate the hope of humanity. And that is the mark of a great photographer.

Therefore there is no paradox between a photographer placing emphasis on subject matter yet by dint of commitment and understanding revealing a personal life-attitude. All great photographs are made at this interface between reality and subjective response.

Chapter 4

Art, And Why It Is So Different

If it is practiced by a man of taste, the photograph will have the appearance of art [but] the photographer must ... intervene as little as possible, so as not ... to lose the objective charm which it naturally possesses.

Henri Matisse

I have come to value photography more and more for those things which it alone can accomplish, rather than to discredit it for the things which can only be achieved through another medium.

Charles Sheeler

Bill Jay: *We have now discussed the fundamental characteristics of photography which make this medium different from all the other visual arts; we have discovered that these characteristics are ideally suited to photography's primary function (to show what something or someone looked like at a precise moment in time) but that this seemingly prosaic function is open to an infinite variety of interpretations; and we have seen that assessing the merit of a photograph also depends on a range of factors so that a good image in one context may be not so successful in another context.*

What we are demonstrating is that the simplest, seemingly most uncontroversial photograph, is likely to present a plethora of complications once it is set adrift into the culture.

David Hurn: To continue this chart of increasing complexity, we will now discuss perhaps the most problematic arena in which photographs can find themselves: fine art.

Photography as fine art is problematic for several reasons. First, when we think of fine art, we tend to think of paintings and the gallery/ museum/collector world in which they operate. But the vast majority of photographs were not intended to, and do not comfortably, fit into this special arena. Therefore some jarring occurs (from both sides) when photographs are exhibited and sold as fine art. Second, the definition of what constitutes art has dramatically changed since photography's invention. Therefore the type of image which was originally considered artistic is vastly different from the ones which now are promoted as fine art. Third, the vast majority of photographs throughout the medium's history have been those that emphasise subject matter (and downplay individuality of authorship), that have been utilitarian, mass-reproduced and functional in society, whereas fine art tends to emphasize originality, uniqueness, the vision of the genius-artist, and its isolation from any utilitarian function.

At the next level of photographic appreciation it is necessary to take some of the implied assumptions in these principles and attempt to clarify them. One of the problems which quickly will be encountered is that the assertions will not allow themselves to be neatly packaged into discrete bits, each following the other in a logical, linear sequence.

There is a good reason for this difficulty.

Students of art history are well aware of the convenience in assigning names to styles in chronological order: neo-classicism — romanticism — impressionism — post-impressionism — cubism — and so on. Such categorization may not be ideal but it is a useful guide for the neophyte.

Unfortunately no such categories can be used in photography. Photography of merit is a mixture of antithetical concerns and styles. More so today than at any time in the medium's history, widely different styles and attitudes comfortably cohabit the field of photography and produce a plethora of diverse images, all of which could be considered as having merit.

By and large, then, photography is bereft of styles, groups, movements, collectives. To be more accurate, such stylistic movements, when they do exist, do not play such crucial roles in the development of photography as they do in painting. As Susan Sontag has written in *On Photography*: "What is most interesting about photography's career ... is that no particular style is rewarded; photography is presented as a collection of simultaneous but widely differing intentions and styles which are not perceived as in any way contradictory."

She is right: it is true, it is interesting, but it is also inconvenient for the person attempting to understand what photographs look like and why they look that way.

In photography we must, at the outset, change one basic assumption otherwise all else becomes impossibly confusing. We must discard the notion that history is linear and consecutive. Photography did not progress along the trajectory of a spear thrust. It was more like the explosion of a grenade, throwing fragments of varying shapes and sizes into a multitude of directions.

A more peaceful, and perhaps accurate, analogy is that photography has grown organically, from a perfectly formed and complete, albeit small, entity to the multi-tentacled and frighteningly complex monster which has now engulfed our society. And like all complex organisms, each body-part has a separate and specialized function. How else can we see bland bank surveillance photographs as part of the same medium as artfully arranged fashion illustrations?

I am beginning to envy the writers of technical how-to-do-it books. There is a simple test for each one of their assertions: if the picture came out, it was good advice: if it didn't, then it was bad advice. No such assurances and simple tests can be made in any discussion on the appreciation and understanding of photographs. I am sure that the previous chapter has left lying around a few bones of contention which will be hotly disputed by the readers. On the whole, however, I think most serious photographers would agree, at least on the basic principles. In the following chapter, no consensus of agreement will be found or expected.

As this discussion of photography, and its meaning, deals with more problematic issues, so the inevitable divisions of attitudes become more pronounced. But this book would not be complete without delving into these hot spots, even at the risk of burning fingers. Working on the principle: nothing ventured, nothing gained, here are a few notes as the basis for discussion and debate.

For the first couple of decades following photography's birth there was little or no discussion concerning the art status of the new medium. Photography was not merely art, it was the finest art. It fulfilled the dream of artists since the Renaissance: the direct transcription of reality. "Note well," emphasized Jules Janin, editor of the influential magazine L'Artiste, "that Art has no contest whatever with this new rival photography, it is not a coarse mechanical invention...No. It is the most delicate, the finest, the most complete reproduction to which the work of man and the work of God can aspire."

Artists, too, were enraptured. The painter Eugene Delacroix wrote in his journal: "How I regret that such an invention arrived so late, I mean as far as I am concerned ... They [daguerreotypes] are palpable demonstrations of drawing from nature, of which hither to we have had only imperfect ideas." Paul Delaroche, one of the most respected artists of the day, declared that "the [photographic] process completely satisfies art's every need, as the results prove."

In response, some of the best known painters of the time abandoned their palettes and reached for cameras. Many of the finer photographers of the early period of the new art were originally painters and their photographs hung proudly alongside paintings in exhibitions and salons. These included Roger Fenton (who studied with Paul Delaroche), Gustave LeGray, Oscar Rejlander, Henry Peach Robinson, David Octavius Hill, and a host of others.

Before long, however, a growing rift widened between painters and photographers. Ironically, the very same ability which initially brought photography its art status (the faithfulness with which it transcribed reality) eventually led to its rejection as a fine art (the production of mere records). If photography was to regain some of its lost prestige as an art, so many practitioners argued, it would need to deny its inheritance as the ideal medium of record-taking, and follow painters in the direction of image-making. Selection from the real world would have to give way to the synthesis or creation of a picture.

Oscar Rejlander was the earliest apostle of this new photographic creed when, in 1857, he constructed an ambitious allegorical picture called The Two Ways of Life from over 30 separate negatives, printed with painstaking care into a single combination print. The result was a deliberate attempt to directly compete with academic painting; it was, and remains, a rare historical curiosity. Rejlander abandoned composite pictures two years later. Henry Peach Robinson became the leading prophet for the new idea, preaching that photography should abandon reality and aim for artificiality and sentimentality.

By the turn of the century, printing processes were available which allowed the photographer more control over the appearance of the image. The gum-bichromate process allowed the photographer to produce images in color, on rough-textured art papers, which were very similar in appearance to crayon drawings, pastels or water-colors. The photographer could even introduce genuine brush-strokes.

These and other attempts by photographers of the past were intended to deny the core characteristics of the medium: the direct recording of a subject with great clarity in a form which could be duplicated conveniently and relatively cheaply. Their aim was a more precious, if not unique, creation which bore the marks of the artist and which shifted emphasis away from the appearance of the subject towards the appearance of the picture itself.

Although these artist-photographers have been given a disproportionate amount of attention in the history of the medium, it should be emphasized that they have always occupied a very small area in comparison with photography in general. If photography, in any age, has been as broad and as long as a football field, then the art-area has been as small as the ball — and it can appear anywhere on the field!

The irony of this situation, and of the shift in the meaning of art in photography, is that prints which are not characteristic of 19th-century work (like Rejlander's) command huge amounts of money at auction, because of their rarity, whereas superb examples of typical Victorian attitudes (like Francis Bedford) can be purchased for absurdly low sums.

This introduction is necessary because photography-as-art has received a growing amount of attention in recent years. Photography's "masterpieces" (the reason why this word is within quotation marks will be apparent a little later) have been selling at auction houses for extraordinary (for photography) high prices, have been assiduously collected by museums and art patrons, and have been reintroduced into smart galleries which in previous decades would have scoffed at mere photographs being treated like fine art.

Feeding and being fueled by this reappraisal of photography-as-art are the growing number of colleges and universities which have included photography in their fine arts programs. In this specialized milieu of art issues it is inevitable that photographers who teach, and are trained, in these institutions view their medium through the very different attitudes and ideals of Fine Art, cutting out of their vision the vast "peripheral" fields of photography which are not relevant to exhibition gallery walls.

And here is the crux of the matter. There is no reason whatsoever why artists should not employ the photographic medium. As a tool of creation the photographic process can take its place alongside the other media employed by the artist, including lithography, etching, drawing, painting, engraving, silk-screen and a host of other processes. However, when photography is employed in this manner by artists, it has moved to the edges of its domain and is best understood through the attitudes, issues and ideas of the academically-trained artists rather than through the principles of photography. This book is concerned with the latter; more general art-appreciation manuals may well be more useful for an understanding of the small specialized area of fine art photography.

In this sense, much of fine-art photography is irrelevant to our discussion. Is photography an art? It can be, when employed by artists — but on the whole, photography is practiced by photographers who have no interest in art issues. In general, photography is *not* art; photography is photography.

I like the story about Edward Weston. A magazine was in the process of publishing an article about him, and sent him the proofs to correct. The magazine had titled the article: Edward Weston — Artist. *On the proof, Weston crossed out* Artist *and inserted the words:* Photographer — and proud of it!

There may be readers of these words who are still puzzled by this seemingly harsh separation between art and photography and who are, perhaps, disconcerted by the statement that photography is not art. The implication, of course, is that if photography is not art then it must be *less than* art. Somehow, through an inexplicable process during the past century, art has risen to the apex of the cultural pyramid. Whether or not it deserves such eminence is debatable. However, it is a common assumption that when photography is criticized for not being art the clear conclusion is that photographs are inferior to paintings or prints. It is worth stressing: photography is not inferior; it is different.

Some of these differences will be self-evident from the previous chapters. In fact, if the basic principles of photography are accepted, it is abundantly clear that photography shares very little with art, in spite of recent improvements in the medium's acceptance by the art establishment. A few more fundamental principles which separate the attitudes of photographers and artists will clarify this point, and then we will return to a closer examination of art-photography as a specialized area within the medium.

Photography was born, as we have seen, in order to record reality with quickness, convenience, accuracy *and in a form which could multiply the image.* Again, the spirit of photography resides as much in the quantity as in the quality of the image, not only in the number of pictures which could be secured of a subject, or at an event, but also in the near-perfect duplication of any particular image.

This asset of photography runs counter to the artist's emphasis on the unique image. Auction houses, museums, and galleries have a vested interest in the single-picture syndrome, the work of art in which resides value, both in the monetary and qualitative meanings of the word. As an example of how these diametrically opposed attitudes have collided in recent years, galleries have often suggested that photographers destroy the negative after a print, or limited edition, has been produced, or at least sign a declaration that no further images will be printed.

A quantity of negatives and the possibilities of an infinite number of positives from any negative have always been at the heart of the body photographic. Therefore it has been essential to judge a photographer by a body of work rather than by a single picture.

Does this mean that the single image has no value in photography? Not at all. There are three major reasons why a single photograph can have great value in the medium:

1. The single photograph is often a potent reminder of the photographer's body of work.

A useful analogy is that the individual pieces of a jigsaw puzzle may be totally incomprehensible when first examined. Once the puzzle has been completed, however, the individual pieces will always have an association with the whole picture. Thereafter, looking at a previously incomprehensible piece will mentally fit into the scheme of the larger interlocked unit and bring to mind the final image.

So it is in photography. A single image may not mean very much when first encountered, but once a larger number of images from the photographer are examined, the single image assumes the role of a mental catalyst, reminding you of the issues embodied in the photographer's work as a whole. The single picture becomes an archetype, a unique representative of the many.

An example might be the famous photograph by Edward Weston entitled Pepper #30. *(Does anyone remember the previous 29 images?) To those familiar with Weston's work, this single picture is a reminder of a period in his life when he was experimenting with a clearer, purer, simple style, by earnestly and compulsively photographing in close-up all manner of prosaic vegetables, fruits and shells. The pepper (#30) is merely one of hundreds of images made during this important time of his life, but stands alone as a potent, and famous, reminder of his still-life period.*

2. The single photograph is often a powerful *symbol* of a social or cultural climate.

Instead of reminding us of the photographer's body of work these symbols remind us of a time in history. No one can predict when such symbols will arise, or even the factors which govern such a selection of a symbol in the collective minds of the public. They just happen, seemingly without warning and often with no reference to the photographer's other work. A vivid example is the extraordinary news photograph of the burning of the airship Hindenburg in 1937. This photograph has become a classic and is used in practically all books of journalism; it is even reproduced in the major history of photography textbook. The image has become a symbol of the death of the dirigible as a passenger-carrying craft. Yet few could even name the photographer (Sam Shere). Even fewer could recall even a single different image from the thousands made by Shere during his 40 years as a newspaper photographer.

There are many other examples. In more recent times, it would be difficult to find an American or European who was not familiar with the image of a Vietnam police officer executing by pistol a captured Vietcong in the streets of Saigon. This photograph by Eddie Adams became a striking symbol of the Vietnam war and probably did more than any other single factor in turning the tide of public attitude against America's involvement in the conflict. Why was this particular image adopted as a symbol? Other photographs were equally shocking in subject matter; many were far more vivid images of death; a great many were much better pictures *than this simple, direct snapshot. Yet a symbol it became — and a classic of its type.*

On the other hand, it is unlikely that it would be included in an anthology or exhibition of great photographs-as-art. It is too closely linked to a specific time, place and political event.

3. The single photograph which is valued may combine both symbolic function and act as a reminder of the photographer's body of work. One photograph beloved by the art establishment is Moonrise Over Hernandez *by Ansel Adams. It may very well be the best-selling art print in the history of photography, each copy selling for thousands of dollars. The image is symbolic of an America at peace, in a time of old-fashioned moral values when life was less complicated; it is also a reminder of Adam's other classic images and his great ability to dramatize the landscape and impart a sense of grandeur and dignity to an otherwise common scene. As a postscript it should be noted that this image also illustrates photography's ability to produce multiples of the same print. A best estimate is that 1,000 prints of this single picture were printed and sold by Adams before his death!*

Back to the problem of understanding the specialized area of art photography. And it can be a problem even for the knowledgeable, sophisticated viewer. There are several reasons for this state of uncertainty.

First, and perhaps most important, most of the museum and gallery photographs are being shown out of context from their original intent. The vast majority of photographers throughout this history of the medium have been working professionals. This is also true of most of the great names of photography in recent decades who have been singled out as artists for the edification of students, who are not informed of the photographers' professional status. These names include Bill Brandt, Ansel Adams, Robert Frank, Garry Winogrand, Elliot Erwitt, Duane Michals, W. Eugene Smith, Walker Evans, Henri Cartier-Bresson, Richard Avedon, Irving Penn, Diane Arbus, Weegee, *et al.* Their photographs were often taken on assignment, for magazines or books, or on advertising or fashion assignments, with not the slightest suggestion of the art-status of their images. Yet in recent years single pictures from their assignments have appeared on gallery or museum walls, carefully and tastefully matted and framed, and discreetly separated from their neighboring images, and presented as individual art objects.

There is no objection to this practice; there are no ethical or critical reasons why photographs should not be used in a variety of contexts. The problem which confronts us as viewers, however, is that we are suddenly asked (because of the art context) to approach the photograph from a mental perspective at variance with the original intent. Occasionally the image slides quite naturally into this role; often, the mental jarring necessary to accomplish the shift leads to confusion.

Here's a personal example. Throughout the late 1950s Robert Frank traveled the length and breadth of America, shooting thousands of pictures of cafe interiors, juke boxes, political rallies, people on the street, urban squalor, street furniture and motor vehicles and so on. Many were shot on magazine assignments. The final selection was presented in a carefully edited and sequenced book, *The Americans*, which has become a classic in 20th-century photography. The book, as a unit, is very powerful. In recent years single pictures have been extracted from the book and exhibited in museums and galleries. Out of context, I find there are not many great pictures and most are rather dull, except as reminders of the whole set; as a unity I think of *The Americans* as one of the most interesting books ever published in the world of photography.

The lesson here is that many photographs may cause confusion when viewed as fine art, because they do not work best under those circumstances. This is not a criticism of those photographs, or of the need for a gallery or museum to emphasize individual works, but merely a recognition that it would be unfair to judge all dogs by the beauty of their feathers.

Another major difficulty when viewing fine-art photographs in galleries resides in their appearance. Often they do not look like photographs at all. These manipulated images are often combinations of processes, with applied color, employing multiple negatives or a wide variety of other techniques and print-making methods. The original subject matter may be totally obscured by style and the picture assumed to be incomprehensible. Yet we have discovered (in the first chapter) that subject matter is of prime concern in photography. Does this mean that such art-photographs can be instantly and totally dismissed as the personal indulgences of artists, of no concern in the medium of photography?

Not necessarily. It is a help, when confronted with such strange concoctions, to remember a simple sentence: although these images may be considered photographs, they are not made by photographers. Therefore the principles of photography as previously outlined do not apply. In order to understand these photographs we must switch to art principles. They are made, discussed, analyzed and judged according to the current standards of art criticism which is very different from the principles involved in general photography. It is as well to remember that artists are at liberty to employ the medium of photography for their own purposes with no regard for this medium's historical origins or intrinsic characteristics. The only difficulty arises when the critical issues of art are applied to non-art photographs and when the critical issues of photography are applied to fine-art photographs. The result is a cacophony of discord of little help to either faction.

This is the very reason why professional photographers tend to view art photographers as self-absorbed dilettantes who have not bothered to learn the fundamentals of their craft but who would prefer to talk aesthetic, academic jargon about their (bad) pictures. Conversely, the artist-photographer often views the professional as an uncultured, if not illiterate, hack who churns out commercial crap like an inferior tradesman. Both viewpoints are misguided.

It would be instructive for every reader to sit in on a discussion about photography with top-flight professionals, such as a group of documentary photographers, followed by a visit to a graduate seminar at a university program in art-photography. I confidently predict that the areas of mutual interest would be nil. It would be difficult to realize that both groups were talking about the same medium. Yet the documentarians could meet with a group of professionals from a widely different area of specialization and find most points in common; the art photographers could meet with a group of print-makers (such as lithographers) and also find most points in common.

For those readers who wish to understand the critical language and aesthetic issues in much of art photography, it is recommended that you read art-oriented books of appreciation and theories of structuralism, formalism, post-modernism and various other -isms of aesthetics. The basic principles of photography do not apply or, to be more specific, their application is not very helpful.

However, there is one fundamental difference between the vast majority of photographs and the small area of art-photography which will help to guide viewers in the right direction. Most photographs, as we have seen, place emphasis on the subject matter seen through the window of the print; most art-photographs place emphasis on the idea of the image reflected from the mirror of the print, to use John Szarkowski's terminology. What this means is that much of art is concerned with problems of perception, aesthetic theories, subjective attitudes of the artist and so on. The emphasis has shifted from the subject to the artist and/or to the process by which photographs are made. They are not intended to be of something but about ideas. And it is helpful to have a prior knowledge of these art ideas when attempting to understand the images.

As a rule, critics are no help in this regard. Their words are often so obtuse that I suspect they too are baffled by the image and hide their bewilderment behind a barrage of art-jargon. And do not forget that much art-photography has no specific meaning which will be unraveled given enough prior knowledge of aesthetic issues. There is no need to feel intimidated when confronted by an unintelligible mixed-media image, because the simple fact may be that the work is stylistically brilliant but utterly devoid of meaning. Its sole function is to act as decor — although artists would cringe at the word. I do not. It seems to me that making pleasant objects with which to adorn a room is a reasonably honorable occupation.

The fact remains that art-photography is a very minor area of photography at large, in spite of its recent over-exposure in the medium, and that it relies primarily on art-issues rather than on photographic principles.

At this point we should face another important aspect of the medium and how it differs from art-as-commodity, and often causes discomfort to the gallery market: so many wonderful images of the past were taken by unknown photographers. If asked who was the most prolific and best photographer in history I would facetiously answer "Anon."

I would not be so facetious, yet answer the same. When I compiled a recent travelling exhibition of my own collection of prints, which I have already mentioned, the unknowns hold their own alongside the others. No question about it. That sort of juxtaposition would be highly unlikely, I think, in an exhibition of paintings which included Renoir, Matisse, Degas, and so on.

I have just been looking through the massive tome, A New History of Photography, *edited by Michel Frizot, and was struck at the number, and quality, of the anonymous images reproduced. It is difficult to imagine that a history of any other visual medium would celebrate the unknown amateur to such a degree. This is an awkward problem for the art market because it runs counter to the prevailing notion that monetary value (equated with merit, unfortunately) is based on the reputation/saleability of the artist's name. I do not think this statement could or would be disputed.*

I can think of a rather boring, by any standard, snapshot of a tree which would be difficult to sell for even a few dollars; but captioned The last photograph I made at Lake George *and signed by Alfred Stieglitz, and the value of the image in the gallery world would be astronomical.*

But even wonderful images by anonymous would not sell very well, unless they were of rare subject matter, such as daguerreotype nudes. Apart from these exceptions, the name is what sells; the anonymous image of merit does not. So the question remains: how and why are some photographers well-known and famous, and sell their images for high prices, while others of equal or higher merit are doomed to a lifetime of obscurity?

It would be nice to think that merit always rose to the top — nice, but not true. Forty years ago there was no art market for photographs because galleries rarely showed them. I remember my first visit to New York City in 1968, when the only gallery exhibiting photographs outside the Museum of Modern Art was in the basement of a private home and was appropriately called the Underground Gallery. I had to make an appointment to see the work on the walls because the owner, Norbert Kleber, earned a living by working in a camera store. Today (certain) photographs are hot sellers at galleries and auction houses, avidly collected by wealthy patrons, museums and institutions. That seems like a wonderful acknowledgement of photography's new-found status in the art world. And so it is. But there is always a price tag, a cost to be paid for any gain.

A few decades ago, without any art-establishment support, photographers themselves were the arbiters of merit. The international community slowly took notice of particularly hard-working photographers and the names would spread until reputations were established after years and years of achievement. Today, many of the arbiters of merit are not photographers. Their intent is the promotion of a saleable commodity, the images of the photographers in their stables. These names may, or may not, be photographers who deserve such recognition. The bottom line is that the most famous photographers today are not necessarily those who are most respected by their peers.

I guess if we partake of the benefits of the consumer society then we have to accept the fact that money, not merit, is the goal. My concern is that these are the images which are collected by major museums, the primary source for future histories of the medium. Therefore a distorted idea of what constitutes the best photography of any period will be created. I cannot believe, for example, that Cindy Sherman's series Film Stills, *bought by the Museum of Modern Art for $1 million, is either worth that amount (compared to other bodies of work by available photographers) or that it represents the finest photography of recent decades. But the series will remain, in a most prestigious and important collection, as a major (and expensive) monument to the medium, and its prominence will ensure that it plays a large part in future histories of this time.*

True, but we want the impossible: a marketplace that recognizes and rewards merit. Impossible. All we can say to a young photographer is: be forewarned and aware that the forces that guide the art-market are business forces, not altruistic or idealistic ones. Do not presume that the famous names are the best photographers — often they are the best promoted photographers. Be critical.

We believe that there is a simple and effective solution to this problem of photography-as-art. We should reserve the term artist as a life-time achievement award, and not use it to describe or identify his/her medium. In other words, a painter is a painter, not an artist, until such times as his/her peers grant this accolade after a life time of achievement at the highest level in the field. Similarly, photographers would only be referred to as artists if the consensus of the field is that he/she deserves the very highest recognition after decades of commitment and achievement.

This makes sense. It makes no sense that a young person of little attainment who has a visual gimmick that is saleable by a gallery should be called an artist. Conversely, a photographer, such as Walker Evans, whose work is archetypically photographic and does not look like art would deserve the honor of being known as a great artist because of the breadth and depth of his achievements.

Chapter 5

Morality, And Why It Is So Important

Photography is a potent medium of expression. Properly used it is a great power for betterment and understanding; misused it can kindle many troublesome fires. Photographic journalism, because of the tremendous audience reached by publications using it, has more influence on public thinking and opinion than any other branch of photography. For these reasons, it is important that the photographer-journalist has (beside the essential mastery of his tools) a strong sense of integrity and the intelligence to understand and present his subject matter accordingly.

W. Eugene Smith

Bill Jay: *I do not believe there is any subject which is off-limits to the photographer. But I do believe that this freedom presupposes a sense of responsibility. An obligation accompanies a right. What I am talking about here is the photographer's moral or ethical sense of right and wrong. Unfortunately this is an aspect of the medium which is rarely discussed but we should emphasize the issue in a separate chapter because it plays a large, but often hidden, part in any viewer's appreciation of a picture.*

David Hurn: What you are really talking about are pictures of people; images of rocks, flower or peeling paint, or any other non-sentient subjects, rarely prompt issues of morality to arise. Although they could. I'm thinking of the sun-bleached cow skull which Arthur Rothstein photographed against two different backgrounds during one of his trips for the Farm Security Administration. As one of them was fake, it brought into question the validity or veracity of all the agency's images of the dust-bowl era — and the resultant scandal nearly brought down the Roosevelt administration.

Nevertheless, pictures of *people* are most likely to cause offense and question the photographer's ethic. So we should start by explaining the beginnings of the problem.

Photography in general received good press throughout the wet-plate era, from the early 1850s to the 1880s. The profession was considered an honorable one; it was useful, enjoyable, and educational. Its applications to both the arts and the sciences were growing, and its public image was held in high esteem. A growing number of well-bred young ladies was entering the profession which was renowned for its lack of sexual discrimination, its rewarding of social skills, and its encouragement of the Victorian virtues of patience, tact and enterprise. The photographic press neverfailingly upheld the respectability of the profession and berated those individuals, or aspects of the trade, which were inconsistent with good manners and a sense of social responsibility. The wet-plate photographer was generally considered to be a respectable member of society.

This image of respectability was quickly lost, never to be recovered, with the advent of the dry-plate and hand camera.

Perhaps if we could have the history of photography all over again, we might decide that the conveniences of the instantaneous picture were outweighed by the trouble it caused; we might decide to stay with the cumbersome, messy, inconvenient wet-plate process. But that is a discussion for another occasion. The fact remains that in all the essays and books on the history of photography in which the introduction of the hand camera is extolled, rarely, if ever, do they recount the social approbation and general distaste directed towards the snapshot. They might point out that the hand camera was scorned by most serious photographers; they do not point out that it was almost universally criticized by every intelligent non-photographer as a major social nuisance. They might discuss the large numbers of amateurs who entered the medium for the first time; they do not reveal that these snapshooters were generally derided as camera fiends. They occasionally mention the competition for already dwindling markets between the professional and the amateur; they do not pursue the idea that the late 19th-century amateur brought photography into such disrepute that it has taken nearly 100 years for the status of (some aspects of) the medium to recover.

To this date the history of photography had never experienced such a shock wave of change.

But what was it exactly to which people objected in snapshot photography that they had not opposed with earlier processes? The answer is straightforward: for the first time people could be photographed surreptitiously. *Of course clandestine pictures had been made with wet-plates (notably in the case of photographing uncooperative prisoners), but these had been the exceptions, necessitating a great deal of prior planning. With the snapshot camera, anyone at any time could be the victim of an embarrassing or even incriminating picture. Sad to relate, the snapshot photographer knew and capitalized on the fact and it became the rage to capture the unposed person in awkward situations. The layman feared and hated the amateur with his ubiquitous camera. And the snapshooters ignored the restraints of common decency and good manners. The problem rapidly reached such proportions that for the first time the act of taking, or not taking, a picture was less an aesthetic consideration and more a moral or ethical one. All the endless debates about the photojournalist and his integrity (or lack of it) during the 20th century up to the present day have their roots in the uninhibited and unconstrained actions of the amateur of the 1880s. Issues were raised at this period which have never, and perhaps never will be, resolved due to the infinite varieties of motives from which pictures are made and of the complexities of personal integrity. However, no discussion of the appreciation of photography would be complete without at least raising the thorny issues of ethics and integrity.*

The plethora of photographs in our culture has swamped our critical faculties; we assume that every facet of life is fair game for the camera, if only to appease our curiosity for a mere second or two. Yet, when viewing photographs, it is valuable to stop and ponder for a moment not only the motives of the photographer but also our motives as onlookers. And it is certainly legitimate to question the tact, taste, good manners and integrity of the photographer when we are presented with the results of his/her behavior in the form of published or exhibited images.

We have compiled a short list of specific cases each one of which demonstrates an ethical question which could be hotly discussed by photographers and viewers of photographs.

1. This is a true story. A photographer was asleep next to his wife. The bedside telephone rang. He switched on the lamp, listened to the voice on the other end of the line, then asked the caller to hold on and placed the receiver on the table. He left the bedroom and returned with his camera. After taking an exposure reading, setting the controls and focusing on his wife, he woke her up and told her the call was for her. He photographed her changes of expression and distress as she was told by the caller that her mother had just died.

Does this incident reflect an admirable commitment on the part of the photographer to record every aspect of life and not only its happier moments? Are we, as viewers of photographs, made more aware of shared emotions, and therefore become increasingly humane by participating in the wife's grief? Or: is this a reflection of gross insensitivity on the part of the photographer who was uncaringly intruding on his wife's grief merely to take a picture? Does such a picture force us to participate in an act of unfeeling voyeurism? Are there some aspects of life which are too personal to be photographed?

2a. During the last years of her life, Marilyn Monroe participated in a photographic session with the photographer Bert Stern — on the condition that she had control over which of the photographs could be published. Bert Stern agreed to this condition. After Monroe's death, many of the photographs which she did *not* want published were displayed in a major feature in *Esquire* magazine.

Did Monroe's death cancel the agreement and free all the photographs to be used for commercial gain by the photographer? Was our interest, as viewers, in the images more important than Monroe's wishes and a justification for the photographer breaking his word?

2b. If either question prompted a *yes*, then let us consider a similar case. Adolf Hitler never liked to be photographed while he was wearing spectacles. His personal photographer, Heinrich Hoffman, made many pictures depicting Hitler with glasses but never allowed these images to be released to the public. After Hitler's death, *The Sunday Times* published these previously censured photographs.

Was this a case of journalistic enterprise in which the public's right to know about a historical figure obviated any and all ethical considerations? Do we have less concern regarding this case, than in the identical case concerning Monroe, because of our lack of warmth towards the subject, and if so, is there one set of principles for nice people and a different set for nasty people?

3. Many photographers have become (in)famous for their determination and tenacity in hounding celebrities. An example is Ron Galella who became somewhat of a celebrity himself due to his unrelenting pursuit of Jacqueline Onassis. The paparazzi type of photographer has become a prominent aspect of the profession due to the insatiable demand of the public for images of the rich and famous in every conceivable situation.

Does an individual whose exploits, wealth or ability have given them public attention pay a fair price for such notoriety in their lack of privacy? Is it reasonable that the public's appetite for any and all images, no matter how trivial, of the famous individual can cause acute distress to that person?

4. There are religious and ethnic groups whose beliefs are opposed to the idea of being photographed. One example of such a sect is the Amish

people of Pennsylvania, a farming community of Fundamentalist Christians whose faith dictates that image-making is sinful. They explicitly do no want to be photographed. Yet photographers constantly attempt to sneak pictures of these individuals without their knowledge, and photographers boast of their pictures taken at a distance with telephoto lenses aimed out of car windows, with a quick get-away before the subjects could react.

We are all curious and intrigued by customs, habits and lifestyles which differ from our own. Is curiosity a valid excuse for aiding and abetting a deliberate flouting of the subject's religious beliefs? Can it be argued that photography, by informing us of the dress, habits and customs of minority groups, is pulling the world closer to an ideal of the brotherhood of man? Or: are these photographs exploitive in that the photographer gains a reputation (and a pecuniary reward) by stealing images from a subject unwilling to give them?

5. An allied problem for both the photographer and viewer is the fine dividing line between collaboration and exploitation. A subject may be willing to pose (or not object if later informed of an image taken unawares) yet find the ultimate use of the picture to be unfair, degrading or dishonest. This may not be the fault of the photographer who, for various reasons, may not have control over the context in which the image is used. Who, then, is to blame, if anyone?

Let us consider an even finer distinction between collaboration and exploitation in the hope of reaching a practical conclusion. Photographs of naked women are of consuming interest — and not only to males. Women's magazines also publish an inordinate number of female nudes which, in any other context, would be considered titillating, pandering to prurient sexual voyeurism, or even grossly exploitive. But that is another issue. The fact remains that a high proportion of viewers are interested in the unclothed female body. Then why is there a difference between those that are degrading and others that exude a sense of integrity?

The answer to this question will emerge from a careful study of the work of E. J. Bellocq (published under the title Storyville Portraits*) and comparing these photographs to any issue of, say,* Penthouse. *On the face of it, Bellocq's nudes should be far more lascivious than the glamour girls in contemporary magazines in that he utilized as models the prostitutes in New Orleans's brothels rather than the wholesome girl-next-door types beloved of the erotic publications. A deeper look, however, reveals that Bellocq* knew and cared *about his models as individual people; his models seem to have collaborated with the photographer without any sense of exhibitionism because they knew Bellocq for a close and trusted friend.* It shows. *Bellocq photographed his models as warm human beings who merely happened to be in a state of (partial) undress — not as breasts and vaginas with incidental other anatomical appendages.*

There is no substitute in photography for a loving, caring, knowledgeable empathy with the subject in front of the camera. And previously asked questions about the ethical nature of photography usually hinge on this fact. The rightness of a picture relies on the photographer's integrity which, in turn, relies on his/her caring understanding on the subject.

But this is not a guiding text aimed at telling the photographer what should or should not be photographed. The issue, however, does have a bearing on the understanding and appreciation of photographs by the intelligent viewer. Every photograph we view is held forever in our minds. We can never un-see it and forget that it existed. Along with the image itself our minds collect its ambience, flavor, sense of caring (or lack of it), connotations, context and a myriad other impressions and feelings. Each photograph conspires to affect and slightly alter our attitudes and ultimately our acts. The issue is important: do photographs we view "conduce to virtue," to affirm and elevate our life-attitudes, to strengthen the bonds between us as fellow-travelers on the star-ship Earth? Or do they, in the words of a British newspaper pundit, Peter Simple of The Daily Telegraph, *"tempt us, by draining all human feelings from what we see, to find first the world of others meaningless and then ourselves."*

Photography's power resides in its nature to ask such profound questions, *if* we actively take part in the viewing experience. What I mean by this is that most viewers passively accept the given information in a picture, without questioning its moral implications, its relationship to reality or how it has been slanted by caption or context. A few viewers might occasionally question the ethics of the photographer if the image is thought to be invasive, obscene or shocking. Fewer still will reflect on their own reaction to the picture and use it to learn about their own foibles, prejudices, taboos, or sense of morality.

That's true. Yet a viewer's reaction to a photograph is always revealing of his/her state of mind and life-attitude. In this sense, the reaction, verbally expressed, tells the listener a great deal about the speaker, often more than about the image. A vivid example, for me, was a set of prints by Duane Michals, Homage to Balthus, *which I sent to a book publisher with scores of other photographs. Before long, the managing director of the company summoned me to his office and was outraged by the pictures, which show in sequence the back of a woman undressing in front of a passive, seated man in the background. It was difficult to understand the seemingly overheated tirade against these particular pictures — until the publisher revealed that he was a Hungarian Jew and, in his youth, saw young Jewish women rounded up by the Nazis and used as their sexual slaves. These pictures acted as potent catalysts for these searing memories, even though Michals could have had no idea they would be interpreted in this way. All my efforts to persuade the publisher that the photographs had nothing to do with his concerns were to no avail; he was adamant in his refusal to publish them. I left the meeting defeated yet enlightened. I had seen a very human side of an otherwise private, cold executive.*

It is very hard to analyze our own reactions. But the efforts are rewarding. *All* photographs can be instructive about ourselves to a greater or lesser degree. When we look at an image we should consciously ask ourselves: what was the photographer's intent?, how well has this intention been realized?, how has meaning been manipulated by all the factors we have previously discussed? and, in addition, we should ask ourselves: what is my emotional and intellectual reaction to the picture *and what does this reaction tell me about myself?*

And this is true even if the answer is: "I am contradicting myself!" At least a sense of ambiguity, and even tolerance for the different opinions of others, is revealed. I am thinking of those who decried the actions of paparazzi in the wake of Princess Diana's death yet create demand for them by buying magazines primarily for the same type of images; of those who abhor the shameless exhibitionism of the Jerry Springer-type television shows yet avidly watch them; of those who deplore the insecurities and personal inadequacies fostered among young women by the advertising industry yet purchase fashion magazines which promote impossible-to-realize standards of beauty; of those who rail against graphic images of, say, car wrecks in the local newspaper yet stop and stare at an accident in the street; and so on. I am not making judgments but merely indicating that we are a mass of contradictions and hypocrisies, but that knowing this to be so can be therapeutic (dread word!).

We must not forget that photographers are also viewers, of their own as well as other's images. It would be instructive to hear a group of high-level street photographers discuss and debate their justifications of taking pictures of people in public without their knowledge or cooperation. Not that I would expect any definitive answer or even agreement (this is one of those divergent questions) but I do think the issues raised would contribute towards a greater sensitivity and awareness.

Again, the public's reaction to these issues would be interesting to discover, if that were possible. How many, I wonder, would agree that a person owns their own image and therefore all pictures taken unawares are immoral? How many would take the opposite view: a photographic image is merely light reflected from a material object (the person) and it is silly to state that the person owns the light? Between these two extremes the gradations and off-shoots are legion. Recently I was photographing in South Beach, Miami, and several incidents, all minor, prompted a maze of musings in my head. One of them was a (male) photographer trying to discreetly take pictures of a couple of bikini-clad young ladies. He acted nonchalantly, tried several approaches, spent a long time getting closer. Then the women noticed him

— and, to his surprise, began posing for him. He took a picture, quickly lost interest and walked away. I thought of the vicarious thrill of voyeurism as a motive for photography and looking at photographs. The same thoughts were prompted by a local male character who roller-bladed naked, except for a cardboard sculpture around his crotch. Women were digging out their cameras to furtively picture him — but lost interest when this exhibitionist began posing for them.

The last incident was of a different kind. On a street alongside the beach I was curious to see people stop and photograph companions, even their children, on some steps of a house. I asked what was going on. The answer was that these were the steps on which Versace was murdered. Some were even looking for bloodstains in the stone. I have no idea what this experience meant but it was eerily disturbing. Should I feel equally disturbed when photographing the people themselves?

I feel the same way when photographing people in different cultures especially if I am accused of exploitation or ignorance of experiences different from my own. It does not disturb me and, if I was totally honest about it, I would not do it. Yet I enjoy the act of photographing. At the same time I make no pretense of telling the Truth about the culture. All I can say is: this is what I saw and how I reacted from my own personal point of view. The problem occurs because *viewers* presume a level of truth in a photograph to which I cannot, and do not attempt to, aspire.

That is true of all photography. Images do one thing supremely well: they show me what something or someone looked like, under a specific set of conditions, at a particular time. All else is supplied by the viewer. And the problem for the viewer is an impossible one — how to sort through all the competing influences on meaning and all the personal reactions, both emotional and intellectual, in order to assess the significance of what is seen.

But it is in the confusion, ambiguities and doubts that the secret lies hidden: self-awareness. Looking at photographs with an open heart and mind help us all in the most important quest of all: becoming actually what we are potentially.

LensWork Publishing

ERRATA PG 84: Paragraph 3, line 3, should read:

It does disturb me and, if I was totally honest about it, I would not do it.

Chapter 6

Looking At Photographs

The artist has three main purposes. His simplest purpose is to describe the outer world; his next is to express his feelings about that outer world; and his last is to express his feelings about himself.

John Fowles, *The Aristos*

Now that we have discussed the core characteristics of photography, how meaning can shift and slide around, depending on the image's context as well as the viewer's state of mind, and some of the factors which affect the assessment of merit, it only remains to see how those principles can be applied in practice with a few specific examples. These conclusions have been written jointly and, therefore, do not follow the discussion-format of the previous sections.

What do you say when your are asked to assess or comment on another photographer's images?

This is a common problem for all photographers, even those with a wealth of experience in teaching. At major conferences it is common to witness scores of young photographers with portfolios scurrying after well-known names in an effort to get them to look at (and approve of) the images, while the names are equally adept at avoiding being trapped.

The irony in this situation is that photographers *like* looking at pictures, or should. So why the avoidance? Simply, it is to escape the chore of performing in front of photographs by unknown people with unknown agendas. The fact of the matter is that just because a person is a respected photographer, it does not mean that he/she is capable of talking about photographs. They are two very different skills.

Nevertheless, the chances are that you will be asked, at some time, to comment on a photographer's work. So what do you say?

If you are unsure of yourself and feel you lack the required experience, the honest answer is something like this: "I will happily look at your photographs; I like looking at pictures. But please do not expect me to comment because I do not know you or your concerns." When finished, say "Thank you" with a smile.

If you are expected to give more than this expression of interest, then ask a lot of questions while looking through the prints. "When/where was this taken?", "how do you feel about taking pictures without the subject's knowledge?", "what do you intend to do with the photographs now that you have made them?", and so on. In this way you will at least learn a great deal about the person, who may be very interesting even if the pictures are not.

But ultimately you will be the authority to whom the other photographer looks for guidance. In this case, use the principles in the previous chapters. Understand that whether or not you like the pictures is unhelpful and irrelevant. Gauge the photographer's intent in taking them; this may be self-evident or it might require a question or two. Inevitably there will be a discrepancy between the photographs and the ideal images for the stated purpose. Offer guidance and advice on how to get from *here* to *there*. This advice might be technical or concern issues of presentation or suggestions regarding publication/exhibition. In this way your remarks will be practical, useful and relevant — and, it is hoped, gratefully received. The important point is this: avoid delving into the photographer's state of mind, emotional history, psychological or philosophical attitudes and other issues of deeply personal origin. Why? Because "This is how I feel" is not a solid foundation for photography (which is not a medium that conveys emotional states with any degree of success) and *because there is no response:* you cannot say: "No, you do not feel that way," only: "Your feeling is not conveyed to me through the image."

For this reason, avoid all open critiques, such as are common in photographic/art courses, in which the participants emote, in jargon borrowed from other disciplines, such as psychology, of which they know very little. Helping another photographer to achieve his/her goals is not a therapy session between the ignorant. For the same reason, avoid giving opinions based on *your* prejudices, emotions or past history. These are not germane to the pictures or relevant to anyone but yourself.

HOW TO WRITE OR LECTURE ABOUT PHOTOGRAPHS.

An extension of the above one-on-one assessment of another photographer's work is when you are asked to publicly comment on images to a wider audience. You are now a critic. Unfortunately, the model for a photographic critic is the one who pontificates in academic jargon, who professes to possess superior insight, and who cannot communicate in simple, intelligible, vivid prose. No wonder that such criticism is useless to practising photographers and active viewers. Good critics of photography are much, much rarer than good photographers.

The guiding principles of a good critic should include the following two "do nots":

Do not tell the reader/viewer what *ought* to be liked or disliked, approved of or rejected.

Note: This does not mean that the critic cannot state his/her preferences and prejudices; indeed it is useful to know what photographers and images the writer admires or dismisses, because these opinions about pictures which you already know will tell you how likely you are to agree or disagree with the assessment about images which you have not previously seen. But this is very, very different from insisting that you comply with the judgments of the critic. The responsibility for what you choose to look at and appreciate is yours alone.

Do not judge, ramble, digress, or delve into areas of expertise of which you know very little.

Note: At the time of lecturing/writing, the critic is acting as an authority. Authority implies a relationship between the speaker/writer who knows more and the listener/reader who knows less. This may be a temporary sense of authority but, for that brief time, knowledge, like water, flows downhill. This means that the critic must have superior knowledge or insight which is of value to the audience. These characteristics are not instinctive; they are acquired through a great deal of thinking, reading, looking and listening.

Once the ego and its attendant dictatorial tendencies have been diminished and the store of knowledge increased, the critic can perform one or more of the following functions:

- introduce the viewer to a photographer or images, previously unknown, in order to widen the available pool of visuals that can be employed for information and inspiration.

- use images to affirm the fundamental principles of photography and, by example, indicate how these can be employed by the viewer for more effective and satisfying images.

- reveal the context and relationships between images of different periods and cultures in order to increase understanding of the past and present.

- make connections between photographs and the social, political, cultural, economic, religious, ethical, legal, and scientific fields in which they play a part.

BE AWARE OF THE PRINCIPLES GOVERNING THE APPEARANCE AND MEANING OF PHOTOGRAPHS WHEN ASSESSING AND SELECTING YOUR OWN IMAGES.

Remember that the primary function of a photograph is to reveal what something or someone looked like. Ask yourself: is the most important part of the image (the face, for example, in a portrait) clearly seen and not confused by a similar-toned or distracting background?

Remember that photography is a *picture*-making process. Ask yourself about each and every frame: would the picture be improved in position — up, down, left or right; a fraction of a second earlier/later release of the shutter? In this critical approach to your own images you will learn how to evaluate the images of others, as well as judge the merit of your own.

Remember that a photograph is unable to convey your feelings at the time of taking the picture. A photograph is a potent memory-jogger, which is both its strength and its weakness. Its weakness is that any photograph will powerfully remind us of the experience of facing the scene. We may be tempted to select images because the memory was so powerful and emotional, or because it was a particularly difficult situation and we are proud of our success. Yet we must disconnect these feelings from the viewing process and select images based on a rational, cold-blooded detachment, on a clear assessment of their merit as pictures alone. Find a photographer of high-standing who will help you assess your images from a critically detached point of view.

Remember that all photographs, even our own, act as catalysts for an internal meandering down the labyrinth of our minds. This process may be helpful towards self-knowledge but it is not a meaning that is implicit in the image. Therefore, when others take a similar mental journey, triggered by your image, yet reach vastly different conclusions, they are not wrong and your interpretation right. Once your image is released into the world it can be (and will be) read in a wide variety of ways. That is to be expected.

Remember that you can direct (to some extent) the meaning of your images by carefully analyzing the preferred audience and, therefore, the means of presentation. A photograph will be read very differently when overmatted and hung on a gallery wall compared to when reproduced in a newspaper. A respectful consideration of the viewer and how to reach this audience is incumbent on all photographers.

Remember that you are not alone in coping with these visual problems. It is a fair bet that others are, and have been, struggling with the same issues throughout the medium's history. Use their work as a vast resource. Do not merely look but closely study as many images as possible by other photographers of the present and past. The chances are that the answers to your own questions will be found among them.

Remember that you cannot expect to make great photographs with any regularity. Photography may be a relatively easy field in which to become reasonably competent (compared to, say, playing a musical instrument) but it is very difficult and time-exhausting to become extremely good at it. There is no substitute for hard work, shooting a lot of pictures, and examining them critically. Although comparisons are odious, as the saying goes, it might come as some comfort to know that even great photographers do not expect to produce more than a handfull of exhibition prints per year.

Finally, remember that even photographers are consumers of images most of the time. We are all bombarded with an endless succession of images of which the makers and purveyors do not have our best interests at heart. They exhort us to vote for a particular candidate, care for a specified concern, condemn a people, group or issue, and, above all, to buy an idea or product. Understanding how a photograph operates and the factors which affect its meaning help us all to become self-defense experts in the struggle for our minds, hearts and wallets. Knowledge is power, as the communication gurus are fond of telling us. In this case, they are right. By understanding how meaning can be manipulated we become inured to those who wish to seduce and lie to us. But the opposite is also true. By understanding the amazing, intricate, complex interactions of the photographic image with the human mind we learn tolerance, compassion and the joys of being truly alive.

About the Authors

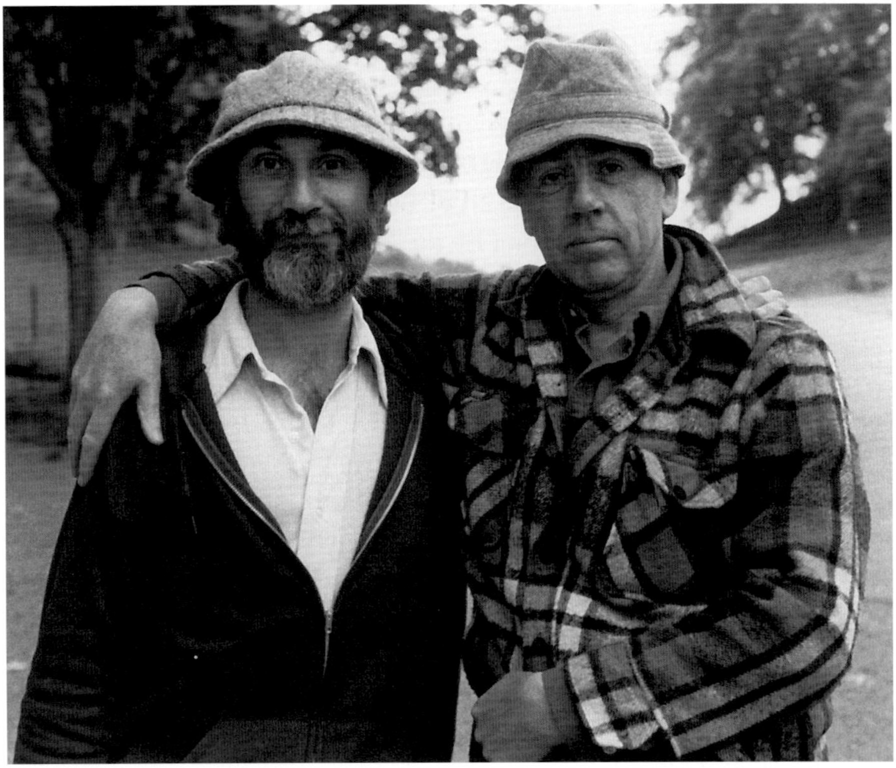

Bill Jay (left) and David Hurn modeling their new Welsh hats

David Hurn

David Hurn has achieved international renown across a wide range of professional photographic activities. As a hard news photographer he cut his teeth at the Reflex Agency as a protégé of Michael Peto. He soon turned freelance and covered major topical events, including the Hungarian Revolution for *Life, The Observer* and major magazines and newspapers throughout the world.

Through his friendship with actors and directors, such as Ken Russell, he began to shoot special projects on major movies, which in turn led to a brief, but lucrative, period as a fashion photographer for *Harpers,The Telegraph* and *Jardin des Modes.*

But it was the feature essay which was his first love and he worked on many assignments concerning what is now known as alternative lifestyles, often with brilliant writers such as Nell Dunne and Irwin Shaw. It was these essays which brought him to the attention of the world's most prestigious photographic collaborative, Magnum Photos Inc. He was invited to become a Full Member in 1967.

In 1970, David Hurn founded one of the most successful experiments in photographic education: The School of Documentary Photography in Newport, Wales. During this time he was active in many institutions promoting photography in Britain, including The Arts Council of Great Britain and The Council of Academic Awards.

Since 1990 he has returned to full-time photography, producing self-assigned major essays for both publication and exhibition. In January 2000 the National Museum and Gallery of Wales honored his images with their Millennium exhibition.

David's latest monograph is *Wales: Land of My Father*, published by Thames & Hudson, London.

Bill Jay

Bill Jay began his career in England where he was the first Director of Photography at the Institute of Contemporary Arts and the first editor/director of *Creative Camera* and *Album* magazines. During this time, he earned a living as Picture Editor of a large circulation new/feature magazine and as the European Manager of an international picture agency.

After studying with Beaumont Newhall and Van Deren Coke at the University of New Mexico, he founded the program of Photographic

Studies at Arizona State University where he has taught history and criticism classes for the past 20 years.

Bill Jay has published over 400 articles and is the author of more than 15 books on the history and criticism of photography. Some of his recent titles include: *Cyanide and Spirits: an inside-out view of early photography; Occam's Razor: an outside-in view of contemporary photography; USA Photography Guide; Bernard Shaw: On Photography; Negative/Positive: a philosophy of photography,* etc.

Bill Jay is a frequent guest lecturer at colleges and universities in Britain and Europe as well as throughout the USA. His own photographs have been widely published and exhibited, including a one-person show at the San Francisco Museum of Modern Art.

David Hurn and Bill Jay have published a companion volume, *On Being a Photographer,* which is available from LensWork Publishing, P.O. Box 22007, Portland, Oregon 97269-2007.

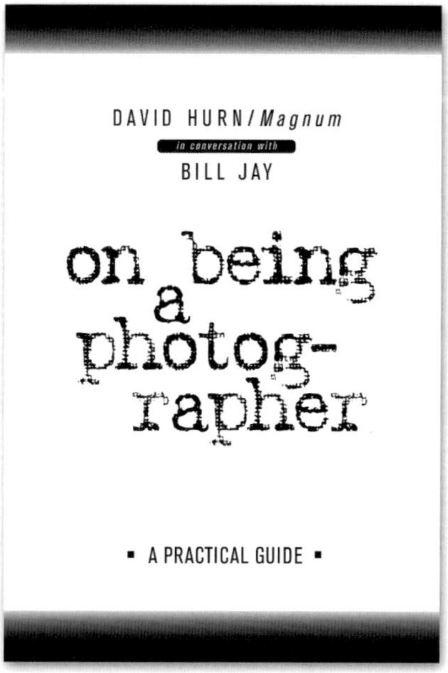

"A very useful book. It discusses issues which will benefit all photographers irrespective of type, age or experience – and it does so in a clear and in-teresting manner. I recommend it."

Van Deren Coke
past Director of
the International Museum of Photography
and author of *The Painter and the Photograph*

"I read *On Being a Photographer* in one sitting. This is an invaluable book for its historical and aesthetic references as well as David's words, which go to the heart of every committed photographer – from the heart of a *great* photographer. It is inspiring."

Frank Hoy
Associate Professor, Visual Journalism, The Walter Cronkite School
of Journalism and Telecommunication,
Arizona State University

"We all take photographs but few of us are photographers. *On Being a Photographer* talks clearly and cogently about the difference ... the book is rich in practical detail about how to practice as a photographer and to create worthwhile pictures."

Barry Lane
past-Director of Photography at the
Arts Council of Great Britain
and presently Secretary-General
of The Royal Photographic Society of Great Britain

David Hurn with Bill Jay, ***On Being a Photographer***.
96 pages, narrative text and interview.
LensWork Publishing, Portland, Oregon.
Third printing, March 2000
ISBN 1-888803-06-1. Paper, US $12.95
www.lenswork.com